Hunting
Pressured Turkeys

HUNTING PRESSURED TURKEYS

Brian Lovett

STACKPOLE
BOOKS

Published by
STACKPOLE BOOKS
5067 Ritter Road
Mechanicsburg, PA 17055
www.stackpolebooks.com

Printed in China

First edition

10 9 8 7 6 5 4 3 2 1

Cover design by Wendy Reynolds
Photographs by Brian Lovett, except where otherwise noted

Library of Congress Cataloging-in-Publication Data

Lovett, Brian.
    Hunting pressured turkeys / Brian Lovett.
       p. cm.
    Includes index.
    ISBN-13: 978-0-8117-3350-2
    ISBN-10: 0-8117-3350-5
1. Turkey hunting. 2. Wild turkey—Effect of hunting on. 3. Wild turkey—Behavior. I. Title.
    SK325.T8L65 2007
    799.2'4645—dc22

                                     2006016352

CONTENTS

ACKNOWLEDGMENTS

I killed my first turkey one April morning in the early 1990s. But my turkey hunting career really didn't start until August 1995.

Pat Durkin, editorial director for Krause Publications Outdoors Group, came to my desk and said he wanted me to be the editor of *Turkey & Turkey Hunting* magazine.

At that time, *T&TH* was co-edited by Jim Casada and Gerry Blair, two of the country's best-known turkey hunting scribes. Gordy Krahn handled in-house duties at Krause's Iola, Wisconsin, office. However, Blair planned to retire at the year's end, which meant a change in leadership for the magazine. Of course, everyone figured Casada would simply take over the magazine's reins, and everything would proceed as it had.

But Durkin and Debbie Knauer, publisher of the Outdoors Division, decided to pull the magazine in-house, and they wanted me to handle it.

I was a bit shocked.

I was already editing *Wisconsin Outdoor Journal,* and I'd been in the magazine business for less than a year. Further, I could count the numbers of turkeys I had killed on one hand, and my calling "expertise" was limited to practicing in my truck with Lovett Williams's Real Turkeys tapes.

Still, I wasn't a dummy. I eagerly accepted, knowing the new duties would mean a lot more work but some potentially great rewards.

During the next seven years, I pretty much received the education of my lifetime. I learned the sacred, time-honored skills of turkey hunting at the feet of the sport's masters. From calling to woodsmanship and everything in between, the turkey hunting industry's pros guided me along the hunter's path. And if I can say I'm a passable turkey hunter nowadays, it's only because those good folks pushed me in the right direction.

I cannot list them all, but here, in somewhat chronological order, are some folks I must thank: Toxey Haas, Ronnie "Cuz" Strickland, Troy Ruiz, Don Shipp, Bob Walker of Alabama, the late Bob Dixon, Greg Neumann, Tom Neumann, Larry Marafka, Harold Knight, David Hale, Mark Drury, Steve Stoltz, John Williams, Jerry Peterson, Gary Sefton, Bo Pitman, Pat Reeve, Mitch McEwan, Tad Brown, Ron Gehrke, Allen Jenkins, David Findley, Brad Harris, Andy Swift, Linda Powell, Ray Eye, Bob Walker of New York, Chad Kilmer, Jim Clay, Tom Duvall, George Mayfield, Brian Pierson, Larry Shockey, Matt Morrett, Alex Rutledge, Dick Kirby, Chris Kirby, Mark Scroggins, Ernie Calandrelli, Al Mattox, Dodd Clifton, Joe Arterburn, Mark Nelsen, Mark Kayser, Wil Primos, Brad Farris, Dan Thurston, Michael Waddell, John Tate, Don and Kandi Kisky, Roger Hook, Mike Miller, Ron and Tes Jolly, C. J. Davis, Jim Crumley, Jerry Martin, Walter Parrot, Keane and Jason Maddy, Steve Coon, and too many others to mention.

During my tenure at *T&TH*, the now-defunct Bass Pro Shops *Outdoor World*, and my latest venture, *Gun List*, I was privileged to work with some of the country's best outdoors writers. Again, I can't name everyone, but suffice it to say, I'm sincerely thankful to anyone with whom I've worked. I have my favorites, of course, whom I must mention by name: Scott Bestul, Michael Hanback, Jim Spencer, Lovett Williams, and the aforementioned Dr. Casada. Thanks, guys, for the treat of reading your stuff.

Special thanks go to Durkin and Knauer, who trusted me with a wonderful magazine and guided me along the way. Thanks to Hugh McAloon, who trusted me with future titles.

I've made some great turkey hunting friendships through the years, including many with folks I just mentioned. Still, I must thank many others, including Jim and Jay Drews, Dan Schmidt, Dick Larson, Al and Jennifer West, Craig Netzer, the Dorshorst family, Dick Hall, Glendon Shearer and family, and the Bestul families of Wisconsin and Minnesota. Special thanks to Jay and Jamie Greene of Crawford County, Wisconsin, and everyone else at the sixth-period turkey camp.

I also want to extend special thanks to Don Gulbrandsen and everyone at Stackpole Books. I sincerely appreciate your faith in me, and thank you for making this process very enjoyable.

Thanks Mom, Dad, Eric (and now Andrea!) for being such a great family. You're the best.

And of course, thank you Jenny for sharing your life with a turkey hunter. I can never thank you sufficiently for your love and support.

INTRODUCTION

I sat at the small table, stumped.

After hearing two or three of what I thought were my best turkey book ideas, Don Gulbrandsen countered with a pretty darned good idea of his own: a book on hunting pressured turkeys.

Hmm. It made sense, of course, but that would be a bit of a departure for me. After all, my theory on pressured turkeys was simple: Avoid them. Find other turkeys to hunt.

But Don elaborated. The topic would work, he said, because many folks cannot simply avoid pressured turkeys or human hunting pressure. They hunt when and where they can, and if that means joining the crowds Saturday morning at the local public hunting area, they do it.

A book on pursuing pressured gobblers would appeal to many folks, he said. With a shrinking hunting land base and growing interest in turkey hunting, it seems to get increasingly difficult to find exclusive access to land or spend time alone in the woods. And let's face it: many folks cannot take chunks of vacation time or spend loads of money to ensure they hunt unpressured birds.

He was right, of course, and I quickly agreed to tackle the book. Still, the topic haunted me for several weeks.

Turkey hunting is turkey hunting, after all. That sounds stupid, but it's true. At its essence, the activity is relatively uncomplicated. It's always difficult, but after you come to terms with that difficulty and reach a certain skill level, you accept that challenge as part of the game. But pressured turkeys? That called for thought (something I also typically avoid).

The more I pondered the idea, the more I began to like it. Also, I began to realize how much human hunting pressure had affected my

With a shrinking hunting land base and growing interest in turkey hunting, it seems to be increasingly difficult to find exclusive access to land or spend time alone in the woods.

turkey hunting endeavors through the years. I started thinking about pressured birds I'd chased and compared them to unpressured turkeys I'd hunted elsewhere. The topic began to take shape in my mind.

I eventually figured out that nothing in this book is ground-breaking stuff. It's simply a text on how to hunt turkeys, sprinkled with anecdotes and examples from my days afield. If anything, the information here is written from a different standpoint than other stuff I've penned. Instead of simply telling you how to call, for example, I took a step backward in the thought process and examined how to call when you're not alone in the woods, and when turkeys have heard nothing but human-made yelps, clucks, cutts, and purrs for several days.

Along the way, I learned to re-examine my entire turkey hunting philosophy, and I really believe writing this made me a better, more thoughtful turkey hunter. (We'll find out in spring!)

Several months after that meeting with Don, that's my sincerest wish for the book: I hope I've provided good, specific information that helps you be a better turkey hunter. Or, more important, I hope it helps you derive more enjoyment from turkey hunting. You won't find all the answers here. Turkey hunting is often too random and unpredictable for that. What I hope you'll find is common-sense guidelines that help you figure out the pressured-turkey mystery on your own.

Read the book, and try to pick up some new pieces to the puzzle. Then, think about how they apply to your hunting situation. Maybe the next time you face one of those do-or-die decisions in the turkey woods— the type that can make or break a morning or even a season—you'll remember a nugget of info that points you in the right direction.

And then maybe, if the stars align, you'll kill that tough old gobbler that's given you fits for a couple of springs. I hope so.

But if that turkey gives you the slip, don't despair. It doesn't necessarily mean you goofed up or failed as a turkey hunter. It probably just means that unpredictable bird did something weird and survived because of it. Keep your chin up, try to learn something from the encounter, and continue hunting.

That might be the biggest lesson in this book: learn, adapt, and keep hunting. I can write thousand of words, and you can digest them all, but the only way to master the challenge of pressured—or any—turkeys is through the school of hard knocks.

So thanks, Don, for the great topic. I hope I've done it justice. And thank you, readers, for your interest. I hope this book serves you well and helps you through the great journey of turkey hunting.

CHAPTER 1

Despite what some folks say, turkeys react and adapt to human hunting pressure. Every critter does, albeit in varying ways.

TES RANDLE JOLLY

Defining a Pressured Turkey

Ah, the good old days. They were simpler times.

Back when turkey hunting was fairly new in my home state of Wisconsin, and I knew even less than I do now, I attended a state-sponsored learn-to-turkey-hunt presentation at a school auditorium. I still remember some of the lessons from that night, including how to cluck on a box call, what a strut zone was, and how turkeys, though they possessed better eyesight than deer, had short memories.

"You can scare a bird away from a field, and he'll have forgotten about it an hour later," the instructor said. "In fact, you can probably set up there again and kill him."

That was all the knowledge I needed.

When April rolled around, a friend and I asked a local farmer if we could hunt turkeys on his property. He agreed, so we made a quick scouting run—without really knowing what to look for—and prepared to hit the woods later that week.

The first morning, we set up in the corner of a hayfield, called a bit, and heard nothing. So we figured we'd head across the road to check out a big corn stubble field. Sure enough, as we topped a small hill, I spotted two or three gobblers strutting for several hens at the field edge. We ducked, but the birds spooked and rubber-necked into the woods.

"No problem," my friend said. "We've got 'em. We'll just go back there tomorrow."

So we did, and soon after daylight, a gobbler and hen appeared over a small knoll and began walking toward us. One of us must have moved because the birds suddenly spooked and flew away.

Shoot. But again, turkeys have short memories, right? No harm done.

As Day 3 dawned, my buddy sat at the same setup, and I watched a small row of cedars across the road. At about 7 A.M., a shot echoed from the stubble field. Soon, I heard another. And another. And another.

Well, at least he'd seen some action.

I abandoned my setup and raced across the road to see my buddy holding up a flopping—and quite dead—gobbler. It was the first turkey either of us had a hand in killing.

"Wow!" I said, spellbound by finally seeing a wild turkey up close. "What happened?"

It had been a classic hunt. My friend, who worked long hours in those days, had walked to the corner of the woods, set out a decoy, called once on a box call, sat down, and fell asleep. He awoke minutes later to the sound of a hen cutting like mad, probably agitated by the decoy. Startled, he moved slightly, and the hen walked away. Just then, he saw the top of a large fan appear above the hilltop. The gobbler had slowly strutted into range by the decoy, and my friend shot him at about fifteen steps. When the bird started death-flopping, my buddy—never having seen that before—put three more rounds into the turkey to finish the deal.

The hunt confirmed everything the instructor had said. We'd spooked turkeys off the field corner two consecutive days, and yet my friend had killed a bird there the third day. Had we been hunting deer or waterfowl, I never would have considered returning to the spot on Day 4. But this was turkey hunting! It was different.

Sure enough, the next morning found me at the corner of the field, with a decoy planted in the stubble and my butt planted by a big white oak. I called once early that morning and then waited for action. And lo and behold, two hours later, a hen appeared ten steps away and walked into my decoys. My heart raced as she pecked her way across the field and into some adjoining timber.

I never had time to catch my breath, either. As I looked away from the hen back toward the corner, four gobblers emerged and began strutting for my decoy. Somehow, I managed to keep it together enough to raise my gun and shoot one. And, when the bird flopped, I shot it again. And again. (Did I mention we were new at this?)

What an accomplishment! We had killed two big longbeards, and from one tiny section of a stubble field. Man, we were turkey hunters. I'd learned the secret formula, and I intended to apply it every subsequent spring. Of course, you've no doubt guessed that's the final time anything like that ever happened.

Oh sure, my buddy killed a jake from the field corner the next spring. But weeks later, I received the first of many tail-whippings courtesy of Mr. Gobbler and was indoctrinated into the world of pressured turkeys.

PRESSURE PRINCIPLES

It's difficult to define pressure and its effects on turkeys. After all, turkeys are a prey species and are "pressured" every day by sharp-toothed critters that want a meal of fresh poultry. Turkeys still thrive, of course, because of their evolution-honed paranoia and powers of survival, including great hearing, incredible eyesight, lack of curiosity, and the ability to get out of Dodge at a millisecond's notice. So, you might say that the constitution and behavior of turkeys is a result of eons of pressure. However, you could say that about any other prey species, too.

The pressure this book deals with comes from clumsy two-legged predators. And despite what my honorable, well-intentioned instructor said years ago, turkeys react and adapt to human hunting pressure. Every critter does, albeit in varying ways. Remember the U.S. soldier who was shot down in the Balkans years ago? He survived by eating ants. When asked afterward about that, he remarked that the more he killed and ate ants, the more difficult they became to catch. If you put predatory pressure on pretty much any species, those critters will react.

Studies in some states have shown that gobbling activity generally decreases—sometimes sharply—after the season opens. Although many factors affect gobbling, you can't overlook the obvious: hunting pressure affects turkey behavior.

That phenomenon is especially evident if you've chased hard-hunted Easterns in Pennsylvania, for example, and then yelped to Rios on an exclusive Texas ranch. It ain't the same game.

Comparing the relative difficulty of subspecies provides insights into pressure. Easterns and Osceolas are often regarded as the toughest subspecies, and Merriam's, Rio Grandes, and even Gould's are considered easier. I've been privileged to hunt all the subspecies, and in my opinion, a turkey is a turkey, no matter where it lives or the coloration of its feathers. They gobble, yelp, strut, breed, and feed. If you move, they're gone. And if a gobbler anywhere is henned up, he's one tough cookie to kill. What's the difference? Pressure. That wary Eastern in Pennsylvania has probably been bumped, boogered, spooked, and maybe even shot at during his brief life. A gobbler of the same age on the South Dakota prairies, however, might have experienced little contact with humans. If everything

Comparing the relative difficulty of subspecies provides insights into pressure. Easterns and Osceolas are often regarded as the toughest subspecies, and Merriam's, Rio Grandes and even Gould's are considered easier. I've been privileged to hunt all the subspecies, and in my opinion, a turkey is a turkey, no matter where it lives or the coloration of its feathers. They gobble, yelp, strut, breed, and feed. If you move, they're gone. And if a gobbler anywhere is henned up, he's one tough cookie to kill. What's the difference? Pressure.

else is equal, that prairie bird will be significantly easier to hunt. He will not have repeatedly spooked because of skulking shadows in the woods or clumsy shining heads that pop up over rises. And if he gobbles at your calling and approaches the "hen," the odds of him being intercepted or boogered by another hunter are slim.

Of course, if every turkey hunter in Pennsylvania said the heck with it and moved to South Dakota, that prairie Merriam's would soon become a far tougher customer. That "hard-hunted" behavior, in my opinion, is simply a function of the human pressure placed on the turkey.

Here's another example, minus the subspecies equation. Hunters generally agree that the best time to hunt Easterns is during the first three to four years the season is open in a specific area. That is, if a new zone in northern Wisconsin opened to spring hunting, birds there would be relatively easier to hunt than turkeys in long-established hunting areas in the southwestern part of the state. However, after that honeymoon period, those previously "easy" turkeys start acting like turkeys everywhere else: difficult. Why? Pressure.

So, it stands to reason that turkeys in the Deep South and Northeast—areas with high human populations and a long turkey hunting tradition—are usually more challenging to hunt than their unpressured cousins. That's also true in many areas of the Midwest, which doesn't have quite the human population as the East but has loads of hunters and a growing turkey tradition.

The nature of modern hunting adds to that phenomenon. Between suburban sprawl and an increasingly privatized rural land base, many hunters are being squeezed out. It's increasingly more difficult to knock on a farmer's door and gain free access to his land. Further, many former farms or rural properties that were once open to everyday folks have been purchased or leased by hunters.

I cannot fault anyone in this. If someone has the means to provide exclusive land for his family and friends, more power to him. And if a hard-working farmer can garner extra income by charging for the privilege to hunt on his land, that's his prerogative. There's no villain. Such scenes are just symptoms of the modern hunting universe. However, many folks—those who can't or won't lease or buy land, and people who have lost hunting spots—feel the squeeze of privatization and must

It stands to reason that turkeys in the Deep South and Northeast—areas with high human populations and a long turkey hunting tradition—are usually more challenging to hunt than their unpressured cousins. That's also true in many areas of the Midwest, which doesn't have quite the human population as the East but has loads of hunters and a growing turkey tradition.

pursue their hunting hobbies on public land or areas where they—and probably other folks—can gain access. As a result, turkeys in those spots experience much more pressure.

But in my opinion, many folks misunderstand how pressure affects turkeys. Let's compare turkeys with other popular game animals. After one or two days of getting banged around your local marsh, most ducks will simply relocate to unhunted waters, or fly only before or after shooting hours. After the opening morning of firearms season in many states, white-tailed deer simply lay low, moving only at night or when absolutely forced to. Pheasants that once held tight for pointing or flushing dogs pile out the far end of a field or marsh when they merely hear a car door slam. And studies in Wisconsin have even indicated that ruffed grouse on small public hunting areas tend to relocate to safe, privately-owned havens after being harassed for a time.

You can't say the same for turkeys. First, because of its nature, turkey hunting—even at heavily hunted areas—doesn't apply the same amount or type of pressure as deer or even bird hunting. On the opening morning of duck or gun-deer season in Wisconsin, for example, you might see fifty or more trucks parked around the outskirts of a small public hunting area. Many private areas aren't exempt, either, as friends and family gather at small farmsteads, or several groups patrol spots owned by a mutual acquaintance.

Even before shooting time, deer are bumped, spooked, and harassed. They're aware that things aren't right, and they immediately change their behavior. After the opening bell sounds, it's not uncommon to hear dozens of gunshots in the first few minutes and steady "snap-crack-pop" action thereafter. If bucks—even does and fawns—can find a safe place to bed down and wait out the din of gunfire, they stick tight to it until they perceive that danger has passed.

Indeed, gun-deer seasons are often an all-out blitzkrieg. Turkey hunting, however, is not. It has fewer participants, which results in fewer gunshots and similar disturbances, so there's far less turmoil in the woods. Now, if 700,000 turkey hunters descended upon Wisconsin's woods for nine days in April (as is the case with the gun-deer season in November), turkeys might act more like whitetails.

But the truth is pressured turkeys are still turkeys. That is, they roost in trees, talk on the roost, and fly down before sunrise. Hens still feed, breed, make nests, and sit on their eggs. Gobblers still strut, spit, and drum, gobble when they're hot, and clam up when they're with hens. If it's hot and sunny, they'll loaf in shaded timber during the day. If it's raining, they're more likely to frequent fields or open areas. If it's windy,

Some hunters talk about turkeys becoming call-shy. This is nonsense. Turkeys do not become wary of or avoid calling. They call and hear calling year-round—from their kin. If they hear a squeaky box call from the same spot ten consecutive days, they do not think, "That's curious. I'd best avoid that area in case that's a hunter trying to kill me."

they'll get out of the wind. In other words, a pressured gobbler won't lie prone in a cedar swamp for ten days like an old, hard-hunted buck. That longbeard is not strikingly different than his unpressured brethren.

If you play your cards correctly and catch him in the right mood during the right day, you can kill him.

WHAT PRESSURES TURKEYS?

Before we look at examples of how turkeys react to pressure, let's discuss what pressures birds.

Some hunters talk about turkeys becoming call-shy. This is nonsense. Turkeys do not become wary of or avoid calling. They call and hear calling year-round—from their kin. If they hear a squeaky box call from the same spot ten consecutive days, they do not think, "That's curious. I'd best avoid that area in case that's a hunter trying to kill me." Even if they hear a glass call that suddenly squeaks, letting out an awful, very "un-turkeyish" noise, they do not think, "Whoa, there's a guy over there with a glass call trying to kill me—and boy is he a crappy caller!" That squeak, no matter how ghastly, is just another noise in the woods to a turkey. They hear strange noises all the time and even gobble at some.

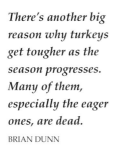

There's another big reason why turkeys get tougher as the season progresses. Many of them, especially the eager ones, are dead.

BRIAN DUNN

As renowned turkey hunter Ray Eye often says, "Turkeys do not get call-shy. They get people-shy."

A turkey—hen, jake, gobbler, whatever—reacts after it's spooked by the same tall, two-legged menace once or twice. When turkey hunters hit the woods opening weekend, they often bust gobblers out of trees, spook strutters in open fields, or startle breeding flocks they encounter while stumbling along in the woods. After a day or two of such encounters, gobbling might decrease, and hunting seems tougher. Because hunters were calling to turkeys, they often believe that the birds have "heard it all" and won't respond anymore. True, the birds have heard it all, but they've heard most of it from other turkeys long before—and after—the season. They're not reacting to the din of box, friction, and diaphragm calling that fills the woods; they're reacting to avoid the tall, even-gaited threats they've encountered.

There is somewhat of an exception to that. If you spook or, worse, shoot at a turkey you've called in, your odds of calling him in again decrease dramatically. Further, your odds of working him from that spot are very slim. But again, that turkey wasn't spooked by the calling. He was probably spooked by movement, a gunshot, or an unnatural situation, such as being able to hear a hot hen but seeing no hen at the source of that calling.

Top: *Turkeys react in varying ways to pressure. If you spook a feeding hen during your morning walk, that turkey probably won't change its behavior much. After all, turkeys get spooked almost daily by what they perceive as predators. But if you bump a gobbler two or three times while traipsing up and down hardwood ridges, he'll likely make himself much more scarce.*
TES RANDLE JOLLY

Right: *Even a turkey that's spooked out of its mind won't "go anywhere." Turkeys have relatively small home ranges, and they don't relocate miles away or migrate like waterfowl to avoid danger.* TES RANDLE JOLLY

If you walk under a roosted longbeard in the dark, it almost always sours his mood somewhat, even if he doesn't spook or flush. So, it stands to reason that birds might be somewhat put off by being spooked repeatedly. But again, they're still turkeys. TES RANDLE JOLLY

At some point after he's spooked, a longbeard will gobble, strut, breed, and feed. And shoot yes, he'll gobble at your calling, too. Further, if you're in the right position and they're in the right mood, you can yelp him in. TES RANDLE JOLLY

Of course, there's another big reason why turkeys get tougher as the season progresses. Many of them, especially the eager ones, are dead. Imagine there are ten gobblers on your hunting property before opening day. If you and your friends kill two hot-gobbling birds the first weekend, you're left with eight remaining birds. If you're fortunate and kill two more the next week, you've reduced the gobbler population by 40 percent. Further, it stands to reason that the easiest turkeys—those that gobbled the best, didn't have hens for some reason, or simply inhabited an area that made them more susceptible to hunting—were among those killed, leaving the toughest turkeys in that remaining 60 percent. That's a vast oversimplification of turkey hunting and population dynamics, but the principle holds true.

Turkeys react in varying ways to pressure. If you spook a feeding hen during your morning walk, that turkey probably won't change its behavior much. After all, turkeys get spooked almost daily by what they perceive as predators. But if you bump a gobbler two or three times while traipsing up and down hardwood ridges, he'll likely make himself much more scarce. And again, if you yelp in a turkey only to spook or miss him, that bird will become much more difficult.

That brings up an interesting point. People often debate the extent to which turkeys learn. They're not geniuses, after all, even when compared to other fowl. Their main survival tools are an incredibly wary nature and razor-sharp senses. Still, it can't be denied that they "learn." If a vehicle drives past a turkey near the road, the bird will usually crane its neck, get a bit nervous, but just wait for the vehicle to pass. But if a person walked by at the same distance to that turkey, the bird would be gone double-quick. The turkey somehow recognizes the difference. However, if someone shot at that turkey from a moving car, it's doubtful the bird would hold still when the next truck passed by. Likewise, a turkey that's been shot at will probably not return to the scene of the crime, at least for a while. I don't know that he necessarily learned to avoid that spot. The gobbler's instincts merely tell it to avoid that area and similar situations. Still, the bird adapted its behavior.

But again, those pressured birds aren't hiding atop trees or skulking behind rocks. They're still turkeys, and they're going to act like turkeys. First, even a turkey that's spooked out of its mind won't "go anywhere." Turkeys have relatively small home ranges, and they don't relocate miles away or migrate like waterfowl to avoid danger. They might shift locales somewhat—roosting a quarter-mile away or avoiding a field or ridge where they were spooked—for a time. However, if not spooked again, they'll probably return to those locations within a couple of days.

It's also true that birds might gobble somewhat less after being spooked. If you walk under a roosted longbeard in the dark, it almost always sours his mood somewhat, even if he doesn't spook or flush. So, it stands to reason that birds might be somewhat put off by being spooked repeatedly. But again, they're still turkeys. They're going to try to breed when the mood strikes them again. That might occur an hour or perhaps three days later, but it's difficult to predict when. After all, numerous factors affect turkey behavior, including weather, phase of the breeding season, and just the plain moodiness of the bird. Human pressure is only one consideration.

Still, at some point after he's spooked, a longbeard is going to gobble, strut, breed, and feed. And shoot yes, he'll gobble at your calling, too. If you're in the right position and they're in the right mood, you can yelp him in just like that unhunted prairie Merriam's I mentioned earlier.

That's what turkeys do. If they didn't, there would be darned few of 'em out there, even in hard-hunted areas. Remember, those areas receive lots of hunting pressure for a reason: there are lots of turkeys there.

So although turkeys certainly react to hunting pressure and change their behavior somewhat—especially in the short term—it's no reason to stop hunting. If anything, you just need to tweak your tactics.

Notes from the Turkey Woods

May 1999

Some turkey hunters are forward-thinking folks. They can probably learn and anticipate events without putting their hand on the proverbial burner.

I ain't in that group. In fact, I'm not even close. But maybe after three days of placing my palm squarely on the red-hot stovetop, I've learned something about pressured turkeys—or specifically, about pressuring turkeys.

I returned to the Dorshorst farm this spring with high hopes. Having honed my skills the past four years with some of the best turkey callers and hunters in the business, I was ready to showcase my calling in a cutting-and-running frenzy. I hadn't had a chance to scout much, but I knew the land fairly well. And besides, after watching how guys like Eddie Salter, Don Shipp, Mark Drury, Steve Stoltz, Harold Knight, Cuz Strickland, and David Hale did their thing, I was convinced my hunt wouldn't last long.

The first morning started perfectly. I listened at a familiar spot, and a gobbler sounded off from the northern ridge—just like birds had always done. I slipped into a setup along the southern ridge and called quietly.

Bam! Three birds hammered from the north, and another joined in from the south. Then, they started gobbling at each other. It was a riot, and I was in the middle of it. I couldn't wait to see which bird would race in first.

I was so juiced up that I disregarded the first few raindrops. The birds continued gobbling, so I figured some wet stuff wouldn't affect anything. But when fly-down time neared and the heavens opened, my heart sank.

I yelped. Nothing.

I clucked. Zip.

I yelped louder. Nada.

My sure thing was being washed away. What would a world-champion caller do? I wasn't sure, so I sat, watching rain drip off my cap, calling now and again in the hopes of provoking a gobble.

After a half-hour, I was wet and perturbed. The turkeys had to be on the ground, but I had no clue where. I couldn't see well through the heavy rain, and I sure couldn't hear much. Sensing that my setup was pointless, I decided to move on and find a better plan.

As I rose to one knee, I glimpsed a flash of white and red 75 yards to the west. Gobbler! No, two gobblers! And they were heading toward me.

The birds hadn't seen me, so I quickly sat and leveled my gun across my knee. Instantly, putting filled the woods. Argh! A third gobbler I hadn't seen had busted me! And every critter in the rain-soaked woods knew the jig was up.

Having honed my skills the previous four years with some of the best turkey callers and hunters in the business, I was ready to showcase my calling in a cutting-and-running frenzy.

God, had I blown it. The rain had made me impatient. I could have stayed put and called sporadically, and those birds would have eventually waltzed in.

But I wasn't too fazed. I had some gorgeous hardwood ridges to walk, and I intended to pound yelps, clucks, and cutting off all of them.

Five hours later, with several miles on my boots, I returned to the fly-down setup. I'd worn circles in my glass call, scraped splinters off my boxes, and blown holes in the latex of my diaphragm calls. In return, I'd called in one group of jakes and a curious raccoon. I was bone-tired and very hungry; it was time for a break.

Out of practice, I cutt loudly on my mouth call before walking into the open. To my astonishment, a bird responded—50 steps away.

I ducked for cover by an old hickory tree and tried to pinpoint the gobbler. Even through the rain, I heard him drumming loudly, yet I couldn't see him. Against my better judgment, I yelped, and the bird gobbled again. He was just out of sight behind a small ridgetop the south. If he merely raised his head for a look, I could shoot him.

The tense standoff continued for a couple of minutes, and the gobbler eventually began to drift to the right.

"Come on," I thought. "Why doesn't he just look for the hen?"

Maybe I got impatient again, or maybe it was an accident. Either way, I moved my body to the right, trying to flow with the turkey, and my vest caught on the tree, sending a loud ripping noise through the woods.

"Putt-putt-putt!"

"No!"

I couldn't believe it. I'd boogered another gobbler. Out of frustration, I cutt, trying perhaps to calm the gobbler down. The bird continued putting and—I swear to God—gobbled between every putt, walking away as fast as he could.

It was finished. Man, I was conducting a clinic.

The next morning, I returned, vowing to hunt smarter and use my head. It was raining and cold again, so nothing gobbled on the roost. Eventually, however, I saw two longbeards follow a pack of hens into the neighbor's stubble field, so I belly-crawled to the property line and tried to call the breeding flock toward me.

It was fruitless, of course, but I sallied forth. One of the gobblers might have lifted his head and looked toward me once, but that was it. They didn't respond and certainly had no interest.

Finally, after an hour or more, the birds wandered into a small woodlot, leaving me alone on my belly in the rain. I spit out my diaphragm call and lowered my head to ease my aching neck.

"Gggaaaaaaaaaarrrrrrrrrrobbble!!!!!!!"

I couldn't believe it. A gobbler had sneaked in behind me. But where was he?

Not daring to move, I peered through the eye slits of my facemask. Of course! He was on that overgrown logging road, just out of sight. I whirled around, sat Indian-style and readied my gun.

"Putt-putt-putt."

Oh no. Nope, he wasn't on the logging road. He was in the small point of woods directly behind me, and I had spooked my third red-hot longbeard—six, actually, if you count the other two the first morning—in a day and a half of hunting.

I could go on about the remaining two days of my hunt, but the story would be pretty boring. The weather got better, but it didn't matter. I'd bumped almost every longbeard on the 200-acre farm, and I don't think I heard another gobble. Those turkeys hadn't been pressured much before then, but I'd sure made up for lost time.

You're probably saying, "Look at the bright side. You learned what not to do." And you're right. Further, I learned that an unfilled turkey tag makes a dandy wrap for a burned hand. ✐

A poor caller who's familiar with his hunting area and turkey movement there will kill more longbeards than a great caller on unfamiliar turf. If you pitted a world-champion caller against a farm kid on land with which the kid was familiar, the smart money would be on the youngster to tote a gobbler back to the barn.

How Turkeys
Use the Land

In our defense, we probably couldn't have done anything differently. Still, it played out like a bad dream.

Oh, it started just fine. As my friend and I listened from a field corner, a solitary longbeard hammered from a hardwood ridge that cut through a cedar swamp. The bird was just off the property we could hunt, but he was very huntable. We hoofed down the field edge, pausing now and then to get a better fix on the bird. After three or four more gobbles, I guessed he was in a thick-limbed oak that bordered a small ridge in the swamp. Further, because of the lay of the land, I guessed he'd pitch toward us.

We eased along as far as possible, finally stopping at a dead tree on the fence line. If we went farther, we'd hit a wide-open area, and the gobbler would surely see us. Although the tree provided sparse cover, the rest of the setup looked good. The bird was 70 yards south of us, and an open, easy hardwood slope extended from the field edge to his tree. I figured he'd hit the ground, walk a few steps to the crest of the small slope, and pop his head up at 25 steps.

Within seconds, the gobbler crashed to the ground. I clucked once on a slate, and he double-gobbled. Perfect. I called twice more in the next two minutes, and he honored every yelp. More perfect. Drumming filled the air, and I listened intently for the bird's approaching footsteps.

But then, a funny thing happened on the way to the kill.

The longbeard started to drift left. He did so slowly at first, so I figured he might just be strutting back and forth, inviting the hen to his domain.

But he quickly picked up the pace, and soon, it was evident that the bird would pop out along the field edge to the east. My friend and I shifted around and got ready, just as the gobbler emerged.

The tom stopped and craned his neck for a moment, searching for the hen. With nothing between him and us—and no decoy out—I figured we were sunk. However, it was still pretty dark, so the longbeard began stepping cautiously into the field, quartering slightly toward us.

I'm not sure what he saw: a shifting gun or two silly-looking blobs hunkered by a dead tree, perhaps. Either way, he soon stopped, periscoped his head, putted once, and turned to leave. He was in range, albeit barely, so I told my friend to shoot. He did, and—using an unfamiliar shotgun—placed a lovely shot string in dirt at the gobbler's feet. The bird jumped in the air and flew a country mile.

It was 5:30 A.M., and our day was done.

After inspecting the scene of the crime, it was easy to see how things had gone wrong. The bird had flown down toward us, as anticipated. Yet instead of hot-footing it up the small rise to our setup, he'd followed a tiny finger ridge from his roost tree to the field. The ridge was just a few feet higher than the swamp and bottom hardwoods it bordered, but to that gobbler, it must have looked like a four-lane highway. As I followed the ridge to the field, I remembered something another friend had told me two years earlier: "They like to pop out in the field here."

Of course. It was just a natural travel area. Though there was no good reason why the gobbler couldn't have come directly to our setup, he was probably accustomed to walking the small ridge to that field, and he'd just done what came naturally.

The only thing we could have done differently that morning would have been to belly-crawl toward the small ridge, anticipating the bird's travel route, but that would have been a huge leap of faith. Or, we could have circled wide around the field and set up at the edge of some pines that bordered the field, hoping to call the bird in after he popped out in the field. Again, that would have been a stretch.

Still, it gave me something to ponder while hunting fruitlessly the rest of the morning.

LANDSCAPE LEARNING CURVE

Most turkey hunters—including me—often underestimate the importance of knowing how birds use the land. Despite their seemingly random behavior, turkeys frequent specific areas for a reason. They don't just walk along a ridgetop on a whim. Their survival or reproductive instincts guided them there.

It's been said a thousand times, yet it bears repeating: A poor caller who's familiar with his hunting area and turkey movement there will kill more longbeards than a great caller on unfamiliar turf. If you pitted a world-champion caller against a farm kid on land with which the kid was familiar, the smart money would be on the youngster to tote a gobbler back to the barn.

Consider Bo Pitman, head guide at the famed White Oak Plantation near Tuskegee, Alabama. He's made a career of putting folks within shooting range of tough southern Easterns, yet—with no offense to him— he's probably a mediocre caller at best. But Pitman maintains an incredible success record by knowing his hunting land and how turkeys use it. As his fellow guides say, he relies far more on his binoculars and seat cushion than on the cracked glass call he carries.

Of course, most turkey hunters gain a general knowledge of their hunting areas, and can pinpoint likely roosting areas, ridges where birds might travel and loaf, and fields or other open areas where turkeys will

Too often, turkey hunters—I'll put myself in this group—think that fancy yelping, the latest decoys, or "secret" calling tactics will lure in a gobbler. They disregard the turkey's natural tendencies and fail to anticipate how even pepper-hot birds react to the landscape and terrain features for specific reasons.

JENNIFER WEST

likely feed and strut. But few consistently connect the dots about why birds frequent some areas, travel certain routes, or use specific areas in certain weather conditions.

If you're a bowhunter, you're likely farther along the learning curve. Because archers must find spots to ambush deer at 30 yards or closer, they pay meticulous attention to the hows and whys of deer location. Further, with few exceptions, they don't fall back on fancy calling or decoys to do that homework for them. Too often, turkey hunters—again, I'll put myself in this group—think that fancy yelping, the latest decoys or "secret" calling tactics will lure in a gobbler. They disregard the turkey's natural tendencies and fail to anticipate—as I did with the missed field gobbler—how even pepper-hot birds react to the landscape and terrain features for specific reasons.

Knowing how turkeys use the landscape might be the Number One skill for killing pressured gobblers. Remember, even heavily pressured turkeys don't vacate their home ranges; they don't go anywhere. They roost in trees, hit the ground in the morning, and feed, breed, strut, and loaf despite the human pressure around them. It's up to you to figure out where they hang out, and then apply those lessons during the season.

The nature of turkey country makes that assignment difficult. After all, turkeys inhabit forty-nine states, several Canadian provinces, and several portions of Mexico. Their "preferred habitat" varies from Deep Southern river bottoms, heavily timbered Northeastern mountains, rolling patchwork Midwestern hills, and the wide-open expanses of the West and Southwest. An Osceola gobbler might spend most of his life in a cypress head and be accustomed to walking through enough water to keep a bass happy. His Nebraska cousin might roost in the same evergreen every night of his life and spend most days frolicking around open range country.

Turkeys evolved as forest birds, so their range always includes trees, albeit far fewer in the West. Much turkey country also features open areas, including meadows, pastures, or agricultural fields. Even large blocks of timber—such as national forests or large mountain ranges—still have small open areas that turkeys use. Further, much of turkey country features some topography changes (that is, hills). This is also an important factor.

Needless to say, it's extremely difficult to categorize and diagram "turkey country." Rather than going state-by-state or habitat-by-habitat, I'll simply try to cover general guidelines and throw in specific examples. Hopefully, you can apply these to your neck of the woods. Please don't consider this the final word on turkeys and the land. Really, it's Turkeys and the Landscape 101. You'll doubtless find exceptions or downright

Turkeys typically roost in relatively large trees. In Texas, a "large" tree might be the only fifteen-foot-tall live oak in a mile radius. Throughout the rest of the country, however, turkeys spend the night in big hardwoods or evergreens. Depending on the size of the tree and the lay of the land, they usually roost fifteen to forty yards high.

contradictions in your hunting areas. But that just further underscores the need for you to formulate your own advanced course of study.

A DAY ON THE LAND

Let's examine how turkeys use the land during a typical day. Basically, this entails roosting, fly-down, feeding and breeding, loafing and fly-up, while considering travel with all these periods.

Determining where turkeys roost might be the easiest task. After all, you'll hear them gobble in the morning; they're providing an aural road map to their location. Also, you might hear them fly up in the evening or down in the morning, and you'll often find wingfeathers and piles of scat under roost trees during the day (more on this in the chapter about scouting).

Turkeys typically roost in large trees. In Texas, a "large" tree might be the only fifteen-foot-tall live oak in a mile radius. Throughout the rest of the country, however, turkeys spend the night in big hardwoods or evergreens. Depending on the size of the tree and the lay of the land, they usually roost fifteen to forty yards high.

In areas with few large trees—Texas, Nebraska, South Dakota, and many other Western states—pinpointing roosting areas is simple. But in

In areas of thicker timber and pronounced terrain, turkeys typically roost two-thirds to three-quarters up—or down, depending on your vantage point—the sides of draws, ravines, ridges, or bluffs. They love to roost off points or knobs that drop off quickly into steep terrain.

the expansive timber of Alabama or unending ridges of southwestern Wisconsin, it becomes more complicated.

Turkeys love to roost in areas that offer them increased safety and advantages for the morning and evening. They often spend the night in trees that overlook a creek, pond, swamp, or drainage. After all, they won't face any terrestrial predators in such spots. They also frequently roost at the edges of fields or meadows, depending on where they feed during the day.

This also lets them simply pitch their wings and sail into a safe open spot right away in the morning. In areas of thicker timber and pronounced terrain, turkeys typically roost two-thirds to three-quarters up—or down, depending on your vantage point—the sides of draws, ravines, ridges, or bluffs. They love to roost off points or knobs that drop off quickly into steep terrain. In very steep country, where deep coulees or drainages climb to flat bluff tops or hightop fields, birds will often roost at eye level to the top, albeit thirty yards up in a tree.

Guessing where turkeys will hit the ground in the morning can be difficult. Usually, it will be relatively open. This lets birds see the spot from their roost tree and provides an easy takeoff and landing zone. They often fly down to the same spot from which they flew up the previous evening. In flat country, they might just set their wings and sail to the woods floor. In open farm country or the prairies, they might sail several hundred feet, resembling mallards as they wing into a field.

Guessing where turkeys will hit the ground in the morning can be difficult. Usually, it will be relatively open. This lets birds see the spot from their roost tree and provides an easy takeoff and landing zone. (They often fly down to the same spot from which they flew up the previous evening.)

In flat country, they might just set their wings and sail to the woods floor. In open farm country or the prairies, they might sail several hundred feet, resembling mallards as they wing into a field. If it's windy during the morning, birds often fly down into the wind, just like a plane landing.

If the landscape has any roll, the equation is easier. Usually, birds fly down to the short side of the terrain. That is, a bird roosted on a hillside will usually sail to the crest of that hill—perhaps eye level for him—rather than flying much farther down to the bottom of the terrain. The short side of terrain simply offers turkeys the shortest distance from Point A to Point B. And if that short side of the terrain has a logging road, open bench, or nifty finger ridge, all the better for turkeys.

Ridges are pretty obvious terrain features, but I think many folks overlook the importance of points, benches, and finger ridges. As their name implies, points are just areas that jut into valleys, ravines, or coulees and drop off quickly to the sides.

After they're on the ground, turkeys pretty much have three concerns: safety, food, and in spring, reproduction. (For gobblers, reproduction basically involves strutting and breeding. For hens, it's more complicated, involving breeding, laying eggs, and nesting, depending on the stage of breeding season.)

Unless hens are nesting, they usually fly down and immediately feed or travel to feeding areas. Gobblers try to stick with hens or, if they're not near any, find them. So it's wise to determine feeding areas and travel routes birds use to reach these. Of course, because turkeys will pretty much eat anything they can fit in their beaks, it's often difficult to guess where and on what turkeys will feed. In farm country, I concentrate on the obvious: agricultural fields and travel areas (ridges, fence lines, and field roads) to them. In thicker timber or areas far from fields, I assume hens will feed on mast or fresh green shoots. So I try to find likely ridges, flats, benches, logging roads, or open areas near roosts. Again, ridges, benches, and roads are also great travel areas, so turkeys might just feed briskly along these paths on their way to fields, meadows, or main ridges.

Ridges are pretty obvious terrain features, but I think many folks overlook the importance of points, benches, and finger ridges. As their name implies, points are just areas that jut into valleys, ravines, or coulees and drop off quickly to the sides. Birds often roost off the tip of points and, assuming they fly down to the point (that is, the short side of the terrain), often travel the crest of that point to a flat, main ridge or agricultural field. Because of the terrain, they often can only travel one direction—straight away from the tip of the point. If you're on a point between a bird's roost and his likely destination, you're in business.

Benches are basically small, flat areas—much like terraces—with open timber along the slopes of ravines, coulees, and hills. Gobblers love to strut in these spots, especially those that receive the first rays of morning sun. If you strike a bird on a hilltop, he's often on a bench.

Finger ridges are basically just smaller ridges that branch from a main ridge. Turkeys feed and strut at these spots, just as they would on a bench or main ridge. They're great travel areas because they offer easy access from fields or lush bottoms to main ridges.

As mentioned, hill, field, and logging roads are always good spots. They often wind from steep areas where turkeys might roost to open

Turkeys—like anything else wearing a dark coat on a sunny day—seek shelter from the heat. They do so by loafing in shaded timbered areas, such as creek bottoms, or flats, benches, ridges, or bottoms with large, shady treetop canopies.

Top: *When it's windy, turkeys generally get out of the wind. Of course, in hilly areas, that could be almost anywhere!*

Right: *During rain, mist, or fog, turkeys often seek open areas, such as fields, meadows, pastures, or thin timber. Why? Who knows? And we can't ask the turkeys. Many folks speculate that rain detracts from turkeys' eyesight and hearing, putting them at greater risk in the woods.*

croplands. Or, they provide easy, open travel areas along steep or thick hillsides. Birds often fly up to and down from their roosts from hill roads.

In very open areas, finding travel routes might not help as much. After all, if birds pitch into a large field and simply walk through the open to their feeding area, there's not much you can do other than figure out where they're going or attempt the belly crawl of all belly crawls (which isn't a good idea in areas with heavy hunting pressure). However, finding open travel or feeding areas might at least let you keep tabs on birds as they move during the day. Eventually, they'll offer you a viable setup option.

As morning wears on, two things occur. First, hens often leave gobblers—briefly in some cases—to lay an egg. Gobblers, of course, try to follow hens to nesting areas, which are often in thicker cover near grassy fields, brushy field edges, or thick draws or ditches. Sometimes, longbeards are left alone, often near the fields, benches, ridges, or roads where their hens left them.

Second, the sun begins to warm the landscape, and turkeys—like anything else wearing a dark coat on a sunny day—might seek shelter from the heat. They do so by loafing in shaded timbered areas, such as creek bottoms, or flats, benches, ridges, or bottoms with large, shady treetop canopies. Sometimes they mill about these spots, pecking or seemingly wandering aimlessly. Often, they squat on the ground, apparently content to wait out the day's heat until evening. In my experience, 70 degrees is often the magic number for loafing. That is, if the mercury hits 70 by about 10 A.M. or so, birds will likely seek shady spots. If it's warm but cloudy, birds seem to tolerate more heat, likely because that nasty sun isn't shining off their dark feathers.

When temperatures subside later, hens usually hit the feed bag again, often working back toward roosting areas. And of course, gobblers follow. As fly-up time nears, birds are usually fairly close to their roosting area. Often, they'll mill about in a staging area near their roost trees before fly-up. Basically, they're just using the landscape as they would in the morning—only in reverse.

As the breeding season progresses, turkeys use the landscape in a slightly different manner. Hens will often spread out and relocate slightly to nesting areas, and gobblers will follow. And when hens are nesting in earnest, gobblers often travel more, walking roads or connecting ridges while trying to find hens still willing to breed.

One final note: Two weather factors play big roles in how turkeys use the land—wind and rain. To me, wind presents the toughest hunting conditions. You can't hear turkeys, and they often can't hear you. Further, the effect of wind on turkey movement is often tough to discern. When it's windy, turkeys generally get out of the wind. Of course, in hilly areas, that could be almost anywhere! They'll often hang out on the leeward slopes of hills or ridges. If it's windy enough, they might hang out in bottoms or valleys. And if it's windy when they fly up, they'll typically roost farther down slopes—even lower in trees—than usual.

Flat, open areas are often windy by nature, and turkeys there are seemingly far more accustomed to breezes. In fact, a 25 mph wind in Texas or South Dakota doesn't seem to affect birds nearly as much as the same blow would in Missouri. Turkeys will still seek leeward slopes or other spots away from the wind, but the equation is much more difficult to figure out.

During rain, mist, or fog, turkeys often seek open areas, such as fields, meadows, pastures, or thin timber. Why? Who knows? And we can't ask the turkeys. Many folks speculate that rain detracts from turkeys' eyesight and hearing, putting them at greater risk in the woods. Others believe moisture spurs them to feed in open areas. Either way, birds frequently hit open areas during and after precipitation.

PUTTING IT TOGETHER

General guidelines are great, but as mentioned, you must put the turkeys-in-the-landscape equation together on your own. There's only one way to do this: hard scouting. It's time to take these Turkeys in the Landscape 101 lessons to your hunting area.

Notes from the Turkey Woods

Bestul's Bold Move

It was one of those mornings when you could feel things going wrong.

The previous two days had been disastrous. My friend Scott Bestul and I had walked miles of southern Minnesota countryside and yelped up a storm searching for a gobbler, only to be beaten down by rain, wind, ice, and uncooperative turkeys.

On the third morning of our hunt, things seemed somewhat brighter when two gobblers hammered from their roost in a deep valley. But when their harem of hens started clucking and yelping, our optimism faded like our white breath on the chilly north wind.

I leaned around the tree and shrugged at Bestul.

"They're just gonna fly down with the hens and mill around," I said.

And sure enough, they flew down with their hens and began to drift toward the other side of the valley.

"Let's get out of here," I said, envisioning another long day of frustration.

"No," Bestul replied. "Come on!"

He shot up from his tree and began charging toward the truck like a man on a mission. What could I do? I followed. Soon, we ducked into Bestul's pickup, and he took off down the road.

"I've seen them do this before," he said. "After they drift up that side of the valley, they get up top on that field and follow the edge toward that little woods you and I hunted a couple of years ago."

Sure, I remembered the little woods. But man, that was a quarter-mile or more from the deep valley where the birds had roosted. Still, Bestul was adamant.

"Maybe it'll blow up in our face, but it's worth a shot," he said.

Again, I couldn't argue. We zipped into the field by the little woods and quickly donned our vests. Bestul led the way, hoofing across a bean stubble field to the edge of the woods.

We crept up to a small rise, and Bestul slowly peeked over the top. Then, he ducked his head and excitedly pointed at the far end of the field.

"There's a strutter with a hen 150 yards away, and he's coming!" he said.

We quickly set up on an old fence post near a dead elm, and I yelped once. A bird gobbled immediately, but it seemed farther than 150 yards away.

"Way off," Bestul said. "There's another turkey in the field!"

Within minutes, the gobbler and hen ran into view. The hen was trotting quickly along a fence line parallel to us at 80 yards. Instead of following her,

Scott Bestul's remarkable plan netted a twenty-five-pound, three-year-old gobbler for the author. Don't ask me why the turkeys wanted to leave that deep ravine and travel cross-country across a beanfield to a tiny woodlot, but they did.

however, the gobbler raced ahead like he intended to cut her off. The longbeard acted so oddly that I thought we might have spooked him. But as they topped the ridge and headed toward the little woods, the gobbler slowed down and broke into strut. I figured he was probably just trying to stay ahead of the hen and gain her attention.

I yelped at the birds once, but they didn't even look up. However, the still-unseen gobbler hammered back just 60 yards away. He was coming right down the field edge to us.

I readied my gun. Seconds later, a huge white head popped over the rise, and drumming filled the air. The bird stepped cautiously ahead, seeking the hen, and then broke into strut. It was time.

I clucked, waited for the bird to raise his head, and fired. The longbeard crumpled, and Bestul and I raced to the scene to celebrate.

Bestul's remarkable plan had come together, and we had a twenty-five-pound, three-year-old gobbler to show for it. Don't ask me why the turkeys wanted to leave that deep ravine and travel cross-country across a beanfield to a tiny wood-lot, but they did. Maybe the hen had a nest nearby, or perhaps there was an irresistible food source somewhere in that area. Whatever the case, that's where she wanted to go, and the gobblers were darn sure going to accompany her.

"I just love figuring out how birds use the terrain," Bestul said later. "Every now and then, you guess right and outsmart one of them."

He was right. Of course, I figure his "guess" was much more the result of smart scouting, hard-learned experience, and keen perception. I was just glad I got to see it firsthand. !く

As old-timers used to say, "Your calling always sounds better if you're where a gobbler wants to go." If you're hunting a new area, maps are good places to start, and you can "map-scout" months before the season, when it's minus 10 outside. Use several sources. Plat books will show you general property boundaries and let you key in on remote areas or tough-to-access properties.

Plan of Attack: Super Scouting and Roosting Methods

It was destined to be a great spring. The season opened Wednesday, but I'd killed my turkey Tuesday.

Now, before you start speed-dialing a Wisconsin conservation warden, let me explain. I'd done my homework so well by Tuesday that killing a turkey Wednesday morning was, in hindsight, pretty much a formality. I'd pegged the birds on my old stomping grounds so well that all I had to do was not screw things up. It was my first truly smart scouting effort.

The Friday before the season, I told my boss I wanted to take the next week off.

"Monday and Tuesday, too?" he said, casting a confused look at me. "You want two days to scout?"

I nodded, and he finally consented.

The request might have seemed odd, but I had never hunted the little farm before, and I needed to learn its ins and outs.

I arrived at the property before dawn Monday, and then hoofed up a logging trail to a likely listening spot. When birds began sounding off from a distant ridge, I sneaked as close as I dared and waited for fly-down. After the birds hit the ground, they shut up, so I stayed put. About ten minutes later, I blew a locator call and received a booming response.

Bingo! The birds had flown down to the ridgetop and drifted westward. I blew the call again, and two gobblers hammered back. I eased a bit closer up the ridge, hoping to keep in contact with what I assumed was a breeding flock but making sure I didn't bump turkeys.

The plan worked perfectly. By using various locator calls, I tracked the birds as they ascended a westward bluff, drifted southward through a hay field, and then seemed to stop and hang out on a long flat atop an east-facing finger ridge.

I carefully slipped behind the flock, mentally mapping out the ridge, crawled up to the hay field, and then gingerly walked along the benches and points that sprawled from the main southern ridge. Then I back-tracked, found the hot roosting spot, and tried to determine where the birds had flown down.

As the sun heated up the morning, I patrolled the property bound-aries, trying to find scratching, dusting areas, and likely-looking benches and flats. It was early afternoon before I quit for lunch. I returned a cou-ple of hours later, hoping to learn where birds loafed during the warm afternoon hours and, later, where they would spend the night. I didn't see or hear any turkeys that afternoon, but I suspected they were probably somewhere along the many shaded flats or bottoms by the main ridge.

About 90 minutes before sundown, I slipped to within 75 yards of where the birds had roosted the previous night. I didn't see or hear any-thing until it was almost dark, when, as I rose to leave, a hen yelped softly from a nearby tree. Contact. No doubt, there was a gobbler or two with her, and they were in the same spot—maybe the same tree—as the night before. I slipped out of the area and drove home, feeling pretty good about the day.

The next morning, rain swept through the area. Had I been hunting, I might have been upset. But for scouting, the scenario was perfect. The turkeys would likely act differently, and I could gain insights about how to hunt the farm during bad weather.

It was raining steadily before dawn, and nothing gobbled. Instead of slipping close to the roost, I hung back by the edge of a large stubble field, figuring—and hoping—turkeys would hit the spot in wet weather. I had to wait more than an hour, but a large breeding flock with two strutters eventually popped out in the northern corner of the field. I watched the birds for a while as they drifted eastward toward a small woodlot and facing ridge. Then I backtracked along their path from the field to the roost and found—surprise—an almost ancient logging road that provided clear sailing from the big timber to the stubble field.

Afterward I walked the property again, eventually sneaking up to the small hayfield, where two hens and a strutter were milling about. Then I sneaked out of the area and headed for home. I would have preferred to return that evening, but the weather was getting uglier, so I figured roosting would be futile. Besides, the birds had roosted in the same spot two consecutive nights, so I had a very good starting point.

When the season opened the next morning, I experienced one of those rare days when everything goes to plan. The birds were right where I expected them to be, and they honored my tree-yelps. Several long-beards flew down pretty much where I'd expected and hammered at my first series of yelps. Two then ran along the southward ridge to my setup, and about ten minutes after shooting hours, I was hoisting a big-spurred gobbler from the woods.

How I wish every spring were like that. Calling might be the essence of spring turkey hunting, but scouting, woodcraft, and woodsmanship have put far more turkey breasts on the grill than the prettiest yelping and hottest cutting.

This is especially true when hunting pressured turkeys. Remember, these birds will be spooked, called at, and perhaps shot at throughout spring, but they won't vacate their home ranges. By gaining intimate knowledge of the land—especially where turkeys roost, feed, travel, strut, loaf, and hang out, and how they'll likely use the terrain throughout the day in various weather conditions—you'll be way ahead of the game. As old-timers used to say, "Your calling always sounds better if you're where a gobbler wants to go."

Let's examine how to formulate and execute a smart pre-season scouting plan, from weeks before the season to the night before your hunt.

GETTING STARTED

You can take your first scouting step—learning about the terrain, timber, and other features of your hunting area—any time before the season, whether it's the previous fall or the afternoon before opening day. However, earlier is better. It's wise to make several scouting forays because you can never know the land too well. Also, in heavily pressured areas, you'll want to stay abreast of human movements and influences on turkeys.

If you're hunting a new area, maps are good places to start, and you can "map-scout" months before the season, when it's minus 10 outside. Use several sources. Plat books will show you general property boundaries and let you key in on remote areas or tough-to-access properties. You can obtain property maps for public land from the regulatory agencies that oversee them. Contact state conservation or natural resources departments for maps to state wildlife areas, or the Bureau of Land Management or U.S.

After you've scoured all you can from maps and photographs, it's time to lace up your boots and hit the scouting road. This will be the most important step in your success or failure with pressured turkeys.

Forest Service for maps to federal lands. Likewise, logging or power companies often have maps available for lands they open to hunting.

Topographical maps are also excellent tools. You can use these to learn about the terrain, entry and exit points, good calling areas, potential calling obstructions, and many more features. Topos are fairly simple to use. Wooded areas are shown in green, open areas are indicated by white, and water is shown in blue. Brown lines show the contour of the terrain. The closer the contour lines, the steeper the country. For example, several long, tightly grouped lines indicate a steep ridge. Conversely, broad, loosely spaced lines show a relatively flat area. Red lines represent boundaries, such as main roads. Secondary roads are shown in contiguous black lines, and broken black lines indicate unimproved roads and trails, including hill roads, logging roads, and power-line cuts.

Also, try to get an aerial photograph of your hunting area (or several, if you're hunting a huge chunk of land). This might reveal features you missed on a topo or property map, including recently logged areas, patches of thick pines, or tiny openings amid timber.

If you have topos, property maps, and aerial photographs, spread them out side by side and compare them. Memorize boundaries, main terrain features, and roads and boundaries within the property. Identify spots you want to investigate, such as long points, finger ridges, timbered flats, creek bottoms, crop fields, and other features.

Also, look for spots that might receive pressure from other hunters. For example, if there's a parking area or county road near a likely looking ridge, you can probably assume there will be a truck parked there opening morning. Don't ignore these spots when you scout and hunt, but make sure you have a back-up plan—better yet, several back-up plans—if your secret spot turns out to be not-so-secret.

After you've scoured all you can from maps and photographs, it's time to lace up your boots and hit the scouting road. This will be the most important step in your success or failure with pressured turkeys.

Again, you can scout land at any time, but it's best to start in late winter or early spring and make several subsequent runs. It's amazing how much more you learn each time you examine an area. Maybe you'll stumble on a small oak-studded flat you missed earlier or find a lush creek bottom full of fresh scratchings.

In addition, starting early lets you learn several areas or properties. It's better to know one area well than to have a cursory knowledge of several areas. But if you have the time and inclination to intensively scout several spots, you'll be better off for it.

Spreading out your scouting runs also lets you better keep tabs on turkeys before the season. For example, by making several trips to an area from late winter until opening day, you can keep tabs on changing turkey locations as spring progresses. As winter wanes, gobblers—and hens, for that matter—begin breaking up and sorting out their pecking order. You'll start to see solo toms, or groups of two or three longbeards, rather than the massive flocks of winter. Subordinate two-year-old gobblers will begin to roost away from their dominant cousins. Hens also spread out as spring breaks, seeking likely nesting areas.

When I walk a property, I'm basically looking for three things: ground-level familiarity with the land, fresh turkey sign, and firsthand knowledge of turkey location throughout the day. After I find these elements, I try to tie them together into a common-sense game plan.

ON THE LAND

With maps and binoculars in hand, I first scout potential hunting areas at midmorning. Usually, I'm scouting these spots long before the season, so I don't care too much about hearing roosted birds. Also, my main goal is to walk the property thoroughly and learn its ins and outs. If I hear or see birds, great. However, I try to make sure I don't bump any, either.

Left: *When I scout a property, I'm basically looking for three things: ground-level familiarity with the land, fresh turkey sign, and firsthand knowledge of turkey location throughout the day. After I find these elements, I try to tie them together into a common-sense game plan.* **Below:** *After I gain a cursory knowledge of the property, I'll return before dawn several days later—usually on what promises to be a good gobbling morning—and listen for turkeys.* TES RANDLE JOLLY

First I'll walk or drive around the property boundaries to make sure I understand them. Then I hit the woods to see how the terrain lays. I'm looking for long timbered ridges, rich creek bottoms, meadows or crop fields, travel areas between spots, and anything that might act as an obstruction when working a turkey.

Ridges offer the perfect scouting venue. Not only do turkeys love to roost just off ridges and hang out there, but these spots often branch off to long points, myriad finger ridges, broad timbered flats, or deep, secluded bottomlands. I'll walk ridges briskly, looking for those spots and also seeking tracks, scratchings, droppings, feathers, or other sign. I also try to "connect the dots" with ridges. That is, I want to see if they connect to fields, secondary ridges, or other features. Further, I examine field edges and other open areas, trying to find travel areas from timber to these spots.

After I gain a cursory knowledge of the property, I'll return before dawn several days later—usually on what promises to be a good gobbling morning—and listen for turkeys. When I hear birds, I immediately try to pinpoint them using my newfound knowledge of the terrain. For example, if I hear a bird gobbling just below a steep ridge, I'll check my maps and memory to see if there's a long point or finger ridge on which the bird might be roosted. Also, I try to see if there's a logging road, open flat, or small meadow where the bird might hit the ground. Often, it takes a few visits and some further investigation to tie this together.

I never use a turkey call when scouting. Why tip your hand or risk calling in a bird and spooking it? However, I'll use locator calls—owl, crow, hawk, coyote, or others—to get birds to gobble after they're on the ground. By doing this, you might keep tabs of a gobbler or breeding flock as they move through the property. For example, if a longbeard hits the ground and later gobbles at your locator call 100 yards down the ridge from where he roosted, he's giving you a clue. Let him drift away, and then check out the area. Chances are, he was on an open bench or small point, hoping to pick up hens. When you locate turkeys in such spots, it's gold.

(Warning: Don't overuse locator calls. If you blow them too much, they lose their shock value. Only use them when you must, and they'll work better for you.)

If birds fall silent as the day progresses, I'll take visual reconnaissance of likely spots, including fields, logging roads, open ridges, or fertile bottomland. If you're lucky enough to see turkeys in the same areas at about the same time two consecutive days, you've found the closest thing there is to a turkey pattern. Combine that sighting with your knowledge of the land, and try to determine what path the birds took to reach that area and

If birds fall silent as the day progresses, I'll take visual reconnaissance of likely spots, including fields, logging roads, open ridges, or fertile bottomland. If you're lucky enough to see turkeys in the same areas at about the same time two consecutive days, you've found the closest thing there is to a turkey pattern.

where they might have roosted the previous night. When you start establishing connections, you're getting ahead of the game.

Basically, I'll continue my scouting visits as often as possible until hunting season. As the opener nears, I pay particular attention to "yelp marks"—that is, evidence of other hunters. If a parking area near a nice ridge is suddenly filled with tire tracks or worse, beer cans, I know there will likely be a camo army there the first morning. Conversely, if I find no tracks or human disturbance along a nifty finger ridge or timbered bench, I'll know those places are probably good spots to start. But either way, I try to formulate multiple plans in case I encounter other turkey hunters. You can never have too many good options during spring turkey season—especially if other hunters are likely to hone in on your options.

IMMEDIATE SCOUTING: ROOSTING

Days before the season, having learned all you can about your hunting area and how turkeys use it, you can set your sights on the ultimate scouting technique: aggressive roosting.

continued on page 44

READING TURKEY SIGNPOSTS

The term "sign" refers to evidence turkeys leave of their presence, including tracks, feathers, droppings, scratching, strut marks, and dusting areas. Here's a brief rundown of what to look for and how to interpret these sign.

Tracks: These are perhaps the most simple, straightforward pieces of evidence turkeys leave. They simply tell you where a turkey was, where it was going, and what gender it was. Typically, the middle-toe tracks of a gobbler measures $2^1/_2$ inches or longer and is markedly longer than the outside toes. Old-timers often joke about a gobbler "giving hunters the finger" with its tracks. Conversely, the toe tracks of a hen are even, with the middle toe being shorter than $2^1/_2$ inches.

Look for tracks along field edges, logging roads, bare ground along ridges, and otherwise moist areas. They might provide clues about where a silent turkey travels after fly-down.

Feathers: You'll often find body feathers here and there throughout turkey country. A black-tipped breast feather, of course, is from a gobbler, and a gold-tipped feather is from a hen. Other than that, body feathers don't tell you much.

However, you'll sometimes find primary wingfeathers (the long ones) near roosts, where turkeys fly up at night and down in the morning. Birds sometimes lose a feather or two when taking flight, so if you find two or three primary wingfeathers—along with multiple droppings—look for likely roost trees nearby. You might have stumbled upon a hot morning area.

Droppings: Generally, the droppings of a gobbler are long and hooked like the letter J. Hen droppings are often smaller, round, and spiral-shaped. (Biologists like Lovett E. Williams, Jr. will tell you that turkeys actually excrete several types of droppings, some of which aren't gender-specific. But for our purposes,

If you find a primary wingfeather, it often indicates a roosting area is nearby.

Reading Turkey Signposts, continued

we'll just focus on the very common, easily discernable hen and gobbler droppings.) Fresh droppings appear moist, and are white with a hint of green. Older scat is dry, hard, and brownish.

Look for droppings near field edges, logging roads, and open ridges. If you find fresh droppings near fresh tracks, you're hot on the heels of a bird. If you find a pile of droppings on the downslope of a ridge, you might have stumbled onto a roost area.

Dusting areas: Like many birds, turkeys take dust baths to clean themselves and rid their bodies of insects and other parasites. They'll use shallow, round areas of exposed sand, dirt, or other soil for dusting, and they do so much more often than people believe.

Veteran turkey hunting scribe Jim Casada once pointed out a dusting area in northern Missouri, and then covered the hen tracks there with his boot. "I'll guarantee you that within a few hours, this spot will be full of tracks again," he said. And he was right. Several dust bowls in an area might indicate hens are nesting nearby. Gobblers won't be far behind.

Strut marks: These are long, straight marks left by a gobbler's primary wingfeathers when he struts for hens. Look for them when you find tracks along dirt roads, field edges, and food plots. If nothing else, they just confirm that an old gobbler is finding hens in that area and will likely try to do so again.

Scratchings: This is my favorite piece of sign. If you find fresh scratching, it indicates turkeys are feeding frequently in an area. Scratchings are basically areas where turkeys have scratched away leaves, duff, grass, or other surface clutter to find mast, seeds, bugs, tubers, or other foods. You'll often find scratching on chufa fields, logging roads, hardwood ridges, areas with mast-producing trees, and loads of other spots.

Of course, turkeys scratch more in early spring, before many of their other food sources—insects, green shoots, and soft mast—are available. You'll often find areas with loads of scratching, indicating large late-winter or early-spring flocks were feeding through a spot. Later in spring, it's more common to find smaller patches of scratching; hens are spreading out, seeking nesting areas. It's pretty easy to discern fresh scratching from old stuff. The exposed soil from fresh scratching will still be dark and moist. Dirt from old scratchings will be dry and hard.

Scratching can indicate the direction turkeys fed through an area. Birds usually make two or three swoops backward with their feet to expose the soil,

When you find a long ridge or green creek bottom full of fresh scratching, mark it with a big red X on your map. Hens are frequenting the area, and gobblers will no doubt be in tow. These are great spots to sit and blind-call when gobbling wanes later in the morning.

and then peck around in dirt. The resulting pile of leaves accumulates toward the direction from which they came; the open, exposed end points toward where they're going.

When you find a long ridge or green creek bottom full of fresh scratching, mark it with a big red X on your map. Hens are frequenting the area, and gobblers will no doubt be in tow. These are great spots to sit and blind-call when gobbling wanes later in the morning.

Roosting a gobbler, of course, means locating him the evening before you intend to hunt. This gives you a huge head-start in the morning and removes any confusion about where to listen or set up. However, there are various degrees of roosting. Sometimes, you might roost a bird 100 or more yards away and have a good idea about which ridge he's on. That's still a great clue for the next day.

But it's far better to know exactly—to the specific limb on the tree—where a bird is. Instead of bumbling around in the dark trying to make an educated guess about where to set up, you know right where to go. Further, close counts in turkey hunting. If you're 60 steps from a longbeard and can see his white head when he hits the ground, that's far better than being 160 steps from a bird and trying to yelp him in.

The best way to "get in the same tree" as a turkey is to roost aggressively, and the folks who perfected this technique are Mark and Terry Drury, of M.A.D. Calls and Drury Outdoors fame. Along with current and former cohorts—Tad Brown, Steve Stoltz, Don Shipp, Steve Coon, Chad Kilmer, John Williams, and many others—these Missouri boys are the best at nailing down gobblers. Mark once told me that if he nailed down a bird at night, he had a better than 50 percent chance of killing it the next morn-

I try to formulate multiple plans in case I encounter other turkey hunters. You can never have too many good options during spring turkey season—especially if other hunters are likely to hone in on your options.

Your scouting should reveal an ideal roost setup—a logging road, open bench, or timbered flat—near the roost tree. Slip in as close as possible the next morning, and call sparingly.

ing. In a sport filled with uncertainties, that's as close as you'll come to a sure thing. Here's how they do it.

Start at about an hour before sunset in good calling/listening areas near spots where you've seen or encountered turkeys. High ridges, knolls, or ravines are ideal because turkeys can hear your locator calling from great distances. Plus you can better hear them. Use loud locator calls. Start with a crow call, and if you receive no response, go to a coyote howler. If that garners nothing, wait a bit, and then try owl hoots near dusk. If that doesn't work, try fly-up cackles on a box or friction call as a last resort.

When a bird gobbles, immediately try to get a general fix on its location. Through your scouting, you'll likely know the bird is near a good-looking knoll, point, or ridgetop. Then, using terrain and foliage, cut the distance at least in half, and call again. If the bird responds, you'll be able to get a better fix on him. Sneak closer again, and try to get another response. If you can get within 60 or 70 yards, you might even get a visual on the gobbler. And if you see him fly up, he's told you where he'll likely fly down the next morning: that exact spot! You might have found your setup.

If the bird gobbles several times, you'll at least be able to determine which tree or group of trees he's in. Then, wait till dark, and slip out of the area. Pay attention to the easiest, quietest route out of the woods. Also, note how long—Mark Drury even counts his steps—it takes you from the turkey to your truck.

Then, make your plan. Use your maps and knowledge of the land to determine where the old bird might hit the ground, how to approach that area, and where to set up. If the gobbler is 50 yards down the slope of a ravine, for example, you can be sure he'll fly down to the short side of the terrain—that is, the high side of the ravine—the next morning. Your scouting should have revealed an ideal roost setup—a logging road, open bench, or timbered flat—near the roost tree. Slip in as close as possible the next morning, and call sparingly.

With luck, you might avoid the pressured-turkey equation and smack Mr. Gobbler in the noggin the minute his wrinkled feet hit the dirt. Then you can walk out of the woods knowing all the hours of reading maps, traipsing through the woods, looking for turkey poop, and roosting birds at night have been well worth it.

Notes from the Turkey Woods

Public Land Longbeards, the Harris Way

Man, Brad Harris, was on a mission.

After two days of fruitless hunting near Mountain Home, Arkansas, we threw our gear in Harris's truck and headed west toward Eureka Springs, where he'd hunted for years. As he drove, I could tell his mental wheels were turning, trying to get us on turkeys immediately.

I didn't consider the move unusual. I was on an "industry" hunt for a turkey magazine, so Harris and I wanted to find the best possible hunting to ensure photos and a story for me and good hunting footage for a video. However, this trip had a twist: we were only hunting public land.

"It'll be a different kind of hunt," Harris had told me days earlier. "Now, it's going to be a challenge; I won't deny that. But it'll be kind of fun to find some spots, try to learn them well, and see if we can't kill a bird there."

And that's what we set out to do. After hunting briefly that afternoon, Harris and I split up to roost birds. We met back at his truck two hours later to compare notes.

"What'd ya hear?" he asked.

I shook my head. Nothing.

"Well, that's all right," he said. "I think I've got something."

After dinner that evening, he spread a topo map on the motel table and spilled the beans. He'd walked a limited-access trail (foot travel only) almost two miles into the property and found a nice green field between two ridges. Then he'd traipsed along both ridges, finding plenty of scratching and a couple of possible roost trees. As darkness fell, he'd owl-hooted from the field edge and heard gobblers respond from each ridge.

"We'll have to get up early to hoof in there, but I don't think we'll need to worry about anyone else," he said. "And if we set up in that field between the birds, I'm sure we can call one into the field."

It sounded so perfect that I wondered what the catch was. But Harris had killed many more turkeys than I had, so I wasn't about to question his plan. We hit the hay early in preparation of an o-dark-thirty wakeup call.

Just a few hours later, after a long walk through the dark Arkansas hills, we stood at the field edge and prepared to set up. I nestled down by a large oak and tried to get comfortable, and Harris and his cameraman settled in behind.

As darkness lifted, a bird gobbled from the ridge in front of us.

"Okay, there's one," I thought.

As if in answer, another turkey gobbled behind us.

"Bingo," I thought. "And we're right between them."

I couldn't see Harris's face, but I'm sure he was grinning as he pulled out his glass call and went to work. Yelps sailed through the air, and both gobblers answered. Then, the birds started gobbling at each other. It seemed like a hallelujah morning.

After the gobblers flew down, the bird behind us gobbled now and then, but the one in front only did so once or twice. I started to worry.

Soon, I realized why he'd clammed up. A black blob appeared at the opposite edge of the field, and a white softball head gazed at us. The turkey had made a beeline to the field!

We hesitated for a moment, wondering whether the gobbler could see our decoys and would commit. When the longbeard broke into strut, we had our answer.

Harris called sparingly, but it was more than enough to keep the turkey coming toward us. The bird went slowly, zig-zagging across the field, alternating between strutting and staring at the decoys. As he walked within 60 steps, the longbeard stopped and gobbled at us, sending shivers up my neck.

Minutes later, he was in our lap, strutting and staring aggressively at our jake decoy. Had I waited for a moment or two, he probably would have thrashed the foam fake. But it was time. As the bird turned sideways and raised his head, I leveled my shotgun bead above his wattles and fired. The gobbler collapsed, ending the hunt.

Harris and I raced 20 steps to the turkey—more for the camera than in any haste—and pulled down our facemasks.

"What a textbook hunt," I said. "Man, everything came together perfectly."

"Well, I didn't get a chance to thoroughly scout this area, but I'd seen enough turkey sign and found a good setup, so I figured our odds were good," he said. "And when those turkeys roosted on opposite ends of the field last night, I was really excited. All we had to do was get between them, and something was going to happen."

It had, and I'd been lucky enough to enjoy the fruits of Harris's two-hour super-scouting job. My only regret was that my shot had gone a bit low, knocking off much of the turkey's once-impressive beard. Still, that was a small price to pay for throwing the Arkansas longbeard over my shoulder. I'd enjoy the walk back to the truck.

But as I turned to leave, Harris smiled, turned the other way and motioned for his cameraman to follow.

"Aren't you heading back for pictures?" I said.

"Yeah, in a while," he said. "It's only 7:30, and that other gobbler is still over here somewhere. I'll catch up with you later."

A quick two-hour scouting session by a friend put the author in front of a public-land Arkansas longbeard. PAT REEVE

With that, he was gone.

Yet as I huffed and puffed the small trail back toward the gate, I was pretty sure Harris would have about twenty pounds of gobbler over his shoulder when he returned. !

CHAPTER 4

Really, calling to pressured turkeys keeps you "real." It makes you think about why, when, and where you call. And it helps you remember that the magical little yelper in your hands or mouth is only one part of a much larger equation.

Calling
Pressured Turkeys

So there I was, six thousand feet up a mountain in Sonora's Sierra Madre Occidental range, ready to yelp, cutt, and cluck my way to a big Gould's gobbler. As a guest of Realtree camouflage, I'd traveled to the turkey camp of Wingshooter's Lodge in Jecora, Mexico, and I couldn't wait to get started.

After all, most of the many gobblers throughout the rugged mountain area had probably never heard a turkey call. Further, I'd hit a groove with my calling and was feeling my oats, so to speak. Hot gobbling action was almost guaranteed.

Two and a half days later, after being beaten up by God knows how many of perhaps the world's least pressured turkeys, I was humbled. I'd blown the reeds out of two or three diaphragms and almost dug a hole in my glass call with only a few courtesy gobbles as my reward. The birds were pretty well henned-up, and I wasn't having any luck with my loud-mouthed approach.

Fast-forward a year later to lower Alabama, home of some of the country's most pressured turkeys. Friend David Findley and I set off on a mission to hunt the infamous "David's Turkey," a bird that had been worked, bumped, spooked, and boogered by some of the best callers and hunters in the country. We figured the old devil would probably gobble once or twice in the tree, fly down, and melt into the thick river-bottom hardwoods. As you've probably guessed, he proved us wrong, gobbling more than a hundred times in an hour and eventually approaching for an iffy shot, which we passed.

Remember two things when calling to turkeys, whether pressured or untouched: emphasize realism, and learn when—and when not—to call.

Such examples could leave you scratching your head. During one hunt, I couldn't call in turkeys that had likely never heard a call. Less than a year later, a tough old gobbler that had heard and ignored the best gobbled his fool head off and played the game like a pepper-hot two-year-old. Maybe those incidents prove nothing other than the fickle nature of turkeys, but I think they illustrate an important point: don't be afraid to call to pressured turkeys. Just use your head.

CALLING REALITIES

As I mentioned in chapters 1 and 3, turkeys don't get call-shy; they become people shy. Sure, studies and personal experience have shown that gobbling often wanes when turkey season opens, apparently in response to hunting pressure. But again, turkeys aren't shying away from all the yelps, clucks, cutting, and kee-kees in hard-hunted areas. They're avoiding the noisy, bumbling two-legged predators that have flushed them from their roosts, spooked them along field edges, bumped them in the woods, and have otherwise raised the alert level in the woods to red. After this occurs, hunters typically hear less gobbling in response to their calling, so they conclude that birds have become wary of boxes, slates, and mouth calls. But it ain't so.

Remember, even hard-hunted turkeys use their natural vocalizations to communicate. Gobblers still gobble to attract hens and assert their dominance over other toms. Hens assembly-yelp to bring their broods together, and poults kee-kee when they're lost. And all turkeys putt when alarmed, cluck when trying to contact other turkeys, and yelp for more reasons than I could list here. If turkeys didn't use these calls, there wouldn't be many turkeys left. And because they make and hear these calls from the day they hatch, they are not alarmed when they hear those sounds, even if those sounds are reproduced poorly.

True, unpressured turkeys usually gobble more and come harder to calling. However, that just reflects their general alert status, not any ignorance of calling. And yes, pressured turkeys often gobble less, hang up more, and are tougher to call in than their unpressured brethren. But again, that's not because they're wary or frightened of the hen calling they're hearing. Whether by nature, circumstance, or reaction to pressure, those birds are just tougher to hunt.

Calling to pressured turkeys keeps you "real." It makes you think about why, when, and where you call. And it helps you remember that the magical little yelper in your hands or mouth is only one part of a much larger equation. It's easy to rely way too much on calling, believing that your seductive notes will overcome poor setups, bad decisions, or ignorance of the terrain. If you assemble the entire turkey hunting package—experience, scouting, calling, and smart in-the-field moves—you'll be amazed at "how good" your calling works. Remember those reluctant Gould's gobblers I hammered with calling for three days? I eventually

True, unpressured turkeys usually gobble more and come harder to calling. However, that just reflects their general alert status, not any ignorance of calling. And yes, pressured turkeys often gobble less, hang up more, and are tougher to call in than their unpressured brethren. But again, that's not because they're wary or frightened of the hen calling they're hearing. TES RANDLE JOLLY

killed one because my Mexican guide set us up in the perfect spot: a low, rocky pasture with a watering hole between two large ridges. After we set up, calling in a bird was simple.

Much of the calling equation is situational, and we'll cover specific examples in subsequent chapters. However, it helps to grasp some basics that apply across the board.

KEEPING IT REAL

Remember two things when calling to turkeys, whether pressured or untouched: emphasize realism, and learn when—and when not—to call.

Realism has many facets. Of course, you want your calling to sound as good as possible. You want it to sound like a real turkey. To do so, you must thoroughly study the intricacies of turkey vocabulary—the sharp pop of cutting, the nasally aspect of kee-kees, or the distinct two notes of a yelp—and learn to replicate those on several devices. You could write a book about how to do this, but the real key is practice and experience. See the sidebars on turkey vocabulary and calling tips. Listen to real turkeys or tapes with real turkey sounds. Attend calling contests to hear what expert-level yelping, clucking, purring, and cutting sounds like. All the while, practice regularly with your calls. Before long, you'll gain a good appreciation of what sounds "turkey" and what sounds fake. And as you become more familiar with your calls, you'll be better able to produce real turkey sounds. Many folks can become proficient with a box call after an hour or two. With friction calls—slate, glass, or aluminum—it might take a little longer. Mouth calls and suction yelpers require more touch and practice, but most folks can operate them sufficiently after some practice.

continued on page 61

In the woods, you're trying to be a turkey killer, not a turkey caller. Calling is just one tool in what should be a large arsenal. When you call, do so for a reason—not to hear your pretty notes or to make up for shortcomings in your comprehensive game plan. This is especially true when chasing pressured birds.

USING THE CALLS

Several thousand years ago, some industrious American Indian hunter learned that if you suck air through a turkey's wing bone, it sounds like a hen turkey. That knowledge probably helped him and his tribe acquire many more turkey bones, but it also spawned the heart of modern turkey hunting: calling.

Although it's not as important as experience and woodsmanship, calling is one of turkey hunting's vital skills. It lets us interact and even communicate with turkeys, which makes turkey hunting unique and enjoyable. Without calling, we'd be reduced to sitting on field edges or attempting to bushwhack gobblers. Here's a quick rundown of the most popular turkey calls and a brief lesson about how to use them. But remember, the key to becoming a good caller is consistent practice. When you hit the woods this spring, your calling skills should be second nature.

Don't Forget Push-Buttons

Often miscast as a beginner's call, the push-button offers great versatility because it's easy to use and great for yelping, clucking, and purring. Push-buttons are ideal for close-range work, mostly because they're not loud and you can operate them with one hand. Traditionally, push-button calls are made of wood. In recent years, however, more manufacturers have offered synthetic models.

To yelp on a push-button call, press the pin steadily but gently—almost to the body of the call—until it produces the two notes of the yelp. Many push-button calls produce better yelps if you operate them with two hands.

Lightly grasp the call with one hand, and gently press on the peg with your other palm. The yelps will sound much smoother. You can easily purr and cluck with one hand. To cluck, press the pin firmly with your index finger, more quickly than when yelping. This produces a short, staccato cluck. To purr, press the pin slowly and steadily.

Box Calls

Boxes probably date back more than 150 years, but they remain a mainstay of modern turkey hunters. Constructed of various domestic or exotic woods, boxes produce great yelps, clucks, and cutting. Experienced callers can also purr well on finely tuned boxes.

The popularity of boxes has suffered during the modern mouth-calling craze. However, as expert callers will attest, you'd be foolish to leave your box calls at home, because they're more versatile than you'd think. Boxes are great for making loud yelps and cutting when you're trying to locate turkeys,

Many people put a death-grip on box calls. Grasp and operate them with a light touch. Also, most boxes sound best when held vertically, not in the palm of your hand.

but they produce soft clucks and yelps equally well when birds are nearby. Further, you can cast your calling by aiming the open end of the box in the direction you want the sound to project.

Many people put a death-grip on box calls. Grasp and operate them with a light touch. Also, most boxes sound best when held vertically, not in the palm of your hand. Lightly grasp the end of the box with one hand—you can hold it with the handle up or vice versa—and then gently hold the paddle between your index and middle fingers. When you run the call, don't lift the paddle off the sounding lid. You'll get a much smoother, more natural yelp. Sure, the paddle will make a soft scraping sound during the upstroke. However, as legendary turkey hunter and caller Ray Eye says, "If a turkey is close enough to hear that, you should shoot him."

If you run the paddle of any box call over its sounding boards, at some point it will break from a high-pitched whistle into the lower, raspier second note of a yelp. Before you try to yelp on a box call, get a feel for how the call "rolls over." Then, speed up the process until you're producing beautiful yelps.

You can cluck and cutt on box calls in several ways. Some folks merely pop the paddle up off the sounding board, producing a cluck. Others lift the paddle and pop it quickly across the board. This is especially good for loud cutting. Further, you can cradle the paddle and box in one hand and then tap the paddle with your other hand, producing clucks and cutting.

One final tip: keep your boxes dry, because a wet box is basically useless.

Mouth Magic

Mouth calls are the darlings of modern turkey hunting, and for good reason. When you hear a champion contest caller blow a diaphragm, it sounds better than any hen that ever lived.

Using the Calls, continued

Diaphragms don't require hand movement, so they're ideal for close work. And they can get loud for striking birds. The main drawback to diaphragms is that you must practice a lot to operate them well. Ray Eye often says using a mouth call is like playing a trumpet. Most people can blow on either and make noise. However, it takes a practiced, experienced operator to make music. (Here's a quick hint: most people blow too hard.)

Before blowing a diaphragm call, get comfortable with it. The cuts in the top reed will always face up toward the top of your mouth. The tab in the frame always goes down. Place the call in your mouth, moisten it, and then press it to your palate with your tongue.

First, make sure it seals okay. Lightly blow air across the reeds, as if you were trying to say "sss." If air escapes from the sides of the call, the diaphragm is not sealing against your palate. Adjust the call until no air escapes.

Practice blowing air through the call until you can make a high-pitched whistle. This is the first note of the yelp. Then, as you whistle, slowly lower your jaw until the sound "breaks," producing the lower, raspier second note of the yelp. Then, coordinate and speed up the process until you're producing sweet, raspy yelps.

After you master the whistle and break of a mouth call, try mouthing "wah, wah, wah" as you yelp. This keeps air flowing over the reed and gives you greater control. Of course, this requires lots of practice. Don't get frustrated. It might take months or even years before you master it.

To cluck on a diaphragm, simply blow a quick blast of air across the reed, as if you were saying "shut." Some folks say "pick" or "pit," but this typically involves too much lip action. Turkeys do not have lips.

To kee-kee on a diaphragm, revert back to your whistle. Make three whistles that ascend in pitch and volume. If you need a trick to better control your air, pretend you're saying "pee, pee, pee."

Purring on a diaphragm can be extremely challenging. Some folks

Diaphragms don't require hand movement, so they're ideal for close work. And they can get loud for striking birds.

Using the Calls, continued

flutter their lips, but most pros blow lightly across the call while gargling in the back of their throats. Even if you master this, your purring might sound more like a cricket. To tone down the sound and better control your air, puff your cheeks as you purr, creating a baffle. That helps you purr softly and sweetly.

No-Restriction Friction

For most hunters, friction calls might be tops. Slate, glass, and aluminum pot-and-peg calls let you hammer out loud cutting or tone down to the softest clucks and purrs. Plus, they're easy to use and might be the most realistic-sounding calls available. Sure, friction calls require some hand movement, but you can easily conceal that by positioning yourself correctly when setting up.

Friction calls have undergone a resurgence in recent years as manufacturers introduce more synthetic calling surfaces. Traditionally, slate and glass were the top choices. After aluminum calls became widely popular in the mid-1990s, however, the market was wide open.

For most hunters, friction calls might be tops. Slate, glass, and aluminum pot-and-peg calls let you hammer out loud cutting or tone down to the softest clucks and purrs.

The striker is equally as important as the call. Some folks like synthetic strikers, especially carbon. Others, however, prefer traditional wood models. As with boxes, make sure to keep wood strikers dry. If they get soaked, the sound they produce will be permanently altered.

When operating a friction call, grasp the pot lightly with your fingertips. Don't set it flat in your palm, because that muffles and stifles the sound. Hold the striker like you would a chopstick, and make sure your hand doesn't rest on the call surface. Lightly touch the striker tip to the calling surface, two-thirds of the way from the center of the call to the edge. Then, drag it across the calling surface in a half-oval, noting where the sound breaks. Without lifting the striker from the surface, pull it back and repeat the process. Soon, you'll be producing sweet yelps.

To cluck and cutt, pop the striker down toward the center of the call. Again, don't lift it from the calling surface.

To purr on a slate, pull the striker lightly toward you. Don't press too hard, or you'll produce a clear note rather than a soft, intermittent purr.

Kee-keeing on a slate is difficult, but good callers make it look easy. Work around the edge of the call, making long drags with your striker. Soon, you'll get a feel for making the long, high-pitched whistles of a kee-kee.

If you don't like the sound of a call at first, experiment with different strikers. Also, vary the pressure you place on the striker. Usually, lighter is better, because you can easily make friction calls "squeak out" by pressing too hard. Some calls respond best to a very gentle touch, but you might need to press harder on others to produce rasp on the second note of a yelp.

Also, experiment to find the "sweet spot" on your friction call. Every call and striker has one. Work several areas around the call, and note which sound best for various calls. It's likely one spot and striker position will stand out from the others. Mark the edge of the call and striker with a magic marker to note these spots.

Totally Tubular

Tube calls don't receive much attention nowadays, but they're valuable turkey tools. They consist of a latex reed stretched halfway inside the opening of a plastic tube. Many old-timers used pill bottles to construct tube calls. Tubes provide two advantages: they're loud, and they offer a different sound than other calls.

To use a tube, hold it to your mouth and rest the bottom edge of the reed on your lower lip. It might tickle, but you'll soon get used to it. Say "tuck" to cluck and cutt. To yelp, blow through the call, and drop your lower jaw

Using the Calls, *continued*

slightly to make the second note of the yelp. Good callers can kee-kee and gobble on tubes.

Wingbone and Suction Yelpers

True turkey addicts love these old-fashioned calls, which produce beautiful turkey sounds. As the name implies, wingbones are made from the wing-bones of turkeys. Suction yelpers operate in similar fashion to wingbones, but they're usually made of wood or synthetic materials.

To operate these calls, hold the end in the crease between your thumb and index finger. Then, press your thumbs together and form a baffle with your fingers. Place the call to your lips, and suck in air—with your mouth, not your lungs—in short gulps, almost as if you are kissing. To yelp, suck in deep gulps. To cluck, take shorter, sharper gulps.

Gobble Calls

These take many forms, but most people are familiar with gobble tubes. To operate these, shake them quickly from side to side, or press them back and forth swiftly between your hands. Gobble calls are useful for challenging boss gobblers or getting hung-up turkeys to respond.

Locator Calls

Whether they imitate owls, crows, geese, hawks, coyotes, woodpeckers, pea-cocks, or any other critter, locator calls are integral elements of any turkey hunter's vest. Basically, locator calls evoke shock gobbles from toms. It's not that turkeys respond to specific critters. They also gobble at airplanes, truck horns, or even shotgun blasts. An old-time hunter once explained shock-gob-bling like this: if you're extremely excited or agitated and someone taps you on the shoulder, you'll likely jump or startle. It's the same with a turkey. If a spring gobbler is revved up with sexual excitement, a sudden loud noise often makes him gobble.

Locator calls are especially handy when trying to find gobblers early in the morning, or when you're trying to move in on a hush-mouthed bird. A word of caution: don't use them too much. A turkey might gobble like mad at a crow call the first three or four times you blow it. If he hears the same crow ten times, however, the shock value will have worn off, and he probably won't respond as much.

A word of warning: some folks have a much higher aptitude for call-ing than others, just as some youngsters are better natural trumpet players than another child. A musically gifted caller might pick up a mouth call and be blowing woods-worthy yelps after a day or two. A relatively tone-deaf hunter might need two or three years of practice to reach the same level. That doesn't seem fair, but it's just the nature of the beast. Don't get discouraged if you're not a "natural" caller. Just keep listening to turkey sounds and continue practicing with your calls. You'll reach a level where turkeys believe you're the real thing, and that's all that matters.

The two other critical aspects of realism are volume and emotion. Con-ventional wisdom holds that when hunting pressured turkeys, it's best to call softly. I won't argue with this, but I think that's somewhat overblown. Turkeys often call quietly, and because they have excellent hearing, have no trouble picking up soft clucks, purrs, and yelps. But turkeys sometimes call very loudly, too, and other birds don't react adversely to that. Why? It's natural.

Gauge the volume of your calling by the situation. Generally, start soft. Unless it's windy or otherwise noisy, turkeys have no problem hear-ing even the softest yelping or purring. Further, if there's an unseen turkey nearby, soft calling won't spook it. Loud calling, on the other hand, could startle a close bird, though I've seen plenty of times when it didn't.

If nothing responds to soft calling, you can increase the volume some-what. If you're walking and calling, for example, try increasing the vol-ume somewhat during your second series of calls and turning it up a bit more for your third series. If you're calling from a setup, wait a bit longer before increasing the volume.

Emotion is somewhat tougher to define. Someone once described it to me like this: if a salesman tried to pitch you something using a flat, mon-otone voice, you'd probably zone him out. However, if his voice was full of life and inflection, you'd probably get the message much better. That holds true with turkeys, too. If you use the same flat set of yelps every time, turkeys don't react as strongly. However, if you make the notes rise and fall, trying to sound like a hen that's anxious to breed, it will likely provoke a much stronger reaction from a gobbler.

Think about a turkey's mood when it uses certain calls. When a bird is cutting, it's excited or agitated. Make your cutting reflect that by vary-ing the cadence, and raising and lowering the volume and pitch. When a hen is clucking and purring, she's usually feeding or otherwise just milling about the woods. Make your clucking and purring soft and almost contented (though purring is really not a call of contentment).

When you set up, think about how to kill the bird, not how to make him gobble a ton. The more a tom gobbles, the better the odds that he'll attract a real hen, or in pressured areas, another hunter.

Likewise, try to reflect the desperation of a lost young turkey into your kee-kees and kee-kee runs, and vary the volume and length of your yelping, trying to indicate agitation or excitement. These are little details, to be sure. However, little details can make a bit difference in the long run.

WHEN AND WHEN NOT
As I mentioned, it's very easy to fall in love with your own calling. If you yelp and a gobbler hammers back, you're inclined to pat yourself on the back and congratulate yourself on a great achievement. Everyone falls into this trap sooner or later—and everyone usually learns the hard way that it's not a wise state of mind.

TURKEY VOCABULARY GUIDE

Turkeys use myriad vocalizations. Here are some of the most common calls:

Cluck: The cluck is one short, staccato note. Often, turkeys will string together two or three single-note clucks. Typically, turkeys cluck to get the attention of another turkey. Some observers say the cluck is the turkey equivalent of saying, "Where are you?"

Putt: The putt is one sharp note. Turkeys usually utter it when they see or sense danger—not to warn other turkeys, but essentially to tell a predator it has been spotted and shouldn't waste its time. Often, turkeys will utter several consecutive putts when alarmed.

Tree yelp: These soft, muffled yelps are the first calls uttered in the morning by roosted birds. Turkeys use tree yelps to communicate with other birds in a flock. They might also cluck softly on the roost and sometimes increase the volume of their tree yelps as fly-down nears.

Plain yelp: The two-note yelp might be the most basic turkey sound. Turkeys often utter series of yelps. The meaning of yelping differs. Turkeys often use yelping to locate other turkeys. Incidentally, hens and gobblers yelp, but a gobbler's yelp is deeper, coarser, and slower-paced than that of a hen.

Cutt: This is a series of fast, loud, erratic clucks, often used by turkeys that are agitated or seeking companionship.

Assembly yelp: Adult hens assemble their broods with a long series of loud yelps.

Cackle: Turkeys usually cackle when flying, whether they're flying up to roost, pitching down in the morning, or sailing across a creek. A cackle usually features three to ten irregular cluck-like notes.

Kee-kee: This nasal, ascending three-note whistle is the basic lost call of young turkeys. A kee-kee run is simply a kee-kee with a yelp or two at the end.

Purr: This is often a soft, rolling call used by feeding turkeys. Some say it's a call of contentment, but most observers believe purring is a call of spatial relations. That is, as a turkey feeds, it tells others in the flock that this is its space. Turkeys also purr aggressively when agitated or fighting for dominance in the pecking order.

Cluck and purr: Feeding turkeys often combine a soft cluck with light purring.

Gobble: The gobble is the only true mating call of the turkey, and it's the main vocalization of the tom in spring. Gobblers gobble to attract hens and assert their place in the pecking order.

In the woods, you're trying to be a turkey killer, not a turkey caller. Calling is just one tool in what should be a large arsenal. When you call, do so for a reason—not to hear your pretty notes or to make up for shortcomings in your comprehensive game plan. This is especially true when chasing pressured birds. Your scouting, experience, woodsmanship, and knowledge of the land are more important than your yelping. Calling is just the final card you play to lure a bird in or make him reveal his location.

And that's really the bottom line when judging when and when not to call: think. Don't use that call until you're ready to make a bird sound off or call him in. If you're walking and calling, make sure you're where a bird can hear you and that you're ready to set up quickly if one responds nearby.

Don't just yelp loudly from the parking lot with no thought about how to approach or set up on a turkey. Likewise, don't call incessantly as you approach a gobbling bird. If you must use hen calling to keep tabs on a longbeard, do it. But only do it as often as necessary, and make sure you're ready to grab a tree and work that bird at a moment's notice. When you set up, think about how to kill the bird, not how to make him gobble a ton. The more a tom gobbles, the better the odds that he'll attract a real hen, or in pressured areas, another hunter. Yes, let him know that hot little hen is ready to breed, and get him fired up. But in general, call only as much as necessary to keep him approaching. (Sometimes you'll call sparingly, but you might call quite a bit in other scenarios. Generally, less is better, but I'll cover the intricacies of working a bird in subsequent chapters.)

I hear what you're saying: those are very general guidelines, and you want specifics, right? Every situation is different, and you could fill a journal with a thousand examples of how varying calling strategies worked or didn't work.

You must gauge every situation individually and fall back on your experience—and sometimes, your instinct—about when and how much to call. Again, less is usually better, but you'll probably note exceptions during your time afield. Just make sure that you have a reason—whether trying to strike a turkey or lure him closer—every time you touch that call.

PRESSURE CALLING

Above all, don't be afraid to use that call, even in pressured areas. Have confidence in your calling, and yelp, cluck, purr, or cluck when the situation dictates. Even if a turkey doesn't respond or come in, it likely won't be because of your calling.

Don't be afraid to use that call, even in pressured areas. Have confidence in your calling, and yelp, cluck, purr, or cluck when the situation dictates.

A MATTER OF COURSE

As a gobble rips through the woods, you temper your excitement with one thought: "Where is he?"

Coursing turkeys—determining which direction a gobble came from, or even nailing down a turkey's location—is an art. Every hunter tries to course gobbling, but some have difficulty doing so, and few are truly skilled at it. Here's a brief primer on coursing gobblers.

The Hearing Factor

Hearing, of course, is the Number One element in accurately coursing gobbles. This isn't a problem for most young hunters. However, as many folks reach their late thirties or forties, they've suffered slight hearing loss. And if they've worked in loud environments, shot without consistently wearing hearing protection, or even hammered on loud turkey calls in confined areas, their hearing might be worse.

Further, hearing loss is insidious. That is, you don't notice it until after it's gone. Often, you'll still hear gobbling, but you can't determine the direction it came from as easily. Obviously, that makes it tough to course turkeys.

Don't despair. If you know you have hearing loss, rely on experience more than ability. A hunter who knows what he's listening for will course birds better than inexperienced folks with superior hearing. And even if you can't determine a longbeard's location after the first gobble, you'll probably get it after the second.

You can incorporate a couple of tricks to improve your odds. Some hunters cup their hands to their ears, which helps them discern gobbles but often makes it tougher to course them. If you can react quickly enough, turn your head slightly as the gobble echoes through the woods. The toughest turkeys to course are usually directly ahead of or behind you. By turning your head, one ear will pick up more sound than the other, and your brain can better determine the origin.

If your hearing has deteriorated so much that you're missing gobbles, consider one of the numerous hearing-enhancement devices available to hunters. Many of these devices also have sound-blocking features that protect your eardrums from loud noises such as gunfire. There's a slight learning curve with these devices. When you first use them, you'll have difficulty determining the direction of enhanced sounds. However, after a while, you'll get a feel for coursing sound just as you would with your natural hearing.

No matter what you're doing—sitting, walking and calling, or just slipping through the woods—always listen intently for turkey sounds that might tip you off.

Firsthand Knowledge

Experienced woodsmen have a huge advantage when coursing turkeys: their knowledge of the land. When a gobbler sounds off, they already have a good idea of where he's at. Of course, that results from scouting and time afield. For example, your pre-season scouting might have revealed an oak flat loaded with fresh scratching. If you hear gobbling from that vicinity later—even if you're 600 yards away—you know it probably originated from the hot flat.

As you scout, note field edges, dusting areas, logging roads, benches along timbered ridges, or other spots you'd expect to find turkeys. When hunting, keep these spots in the back of your mind. If a sudden gobble surprises you, think of the terrain features in that area. You'll be surprised how often you nail down a turkey's specific location from just a gobble or two. Also, you'll have a much better idea how to approach and set up on that bird.

A Matter of Course

No matter what you're doing—sitting, walking and calling, or just slipping through the woods—always listen intently for turkey sounds that might tip you off. Then use your experience to pinpoint and set up on birds. After a while, it becomes second nature. And what if you miscourse a turkey? Laugh it off. It happens to everyone. You'll get the next one.

Notes from the Turkey Woods

The Killing Call of Silence

I was still pretty groggy when Mark Drury woke me up. My flight into St. Louis had been late, as had the planes for two fellow outdoors writers. By the time we'd loaded our gear in a rental car and driven the three-plus hours to Drury's northern Missouri turkey camp near Kirksville, it was early morning.

But three hours of sleep or not, I was going turkey hunting. Mark pointed me toward the coffee and then gently suggested that we needed to make haste.

"We've gotta roll, buddy," he said. "You can take a nap after you kill your turkey." Ah, that's why I like Mark. He's always optimistic. But unlike other turkey optimists, he usually backs it up.

We drove a half-hour through the dark until we rendezvoused with Chad Kilmer, a Drury pro-staffer whose family owns land near Novinger. I shook hands with Chad, mumbled something about the nice morning, and then tried to keep up with two long-legged, well-rested turkey nuts as they hoofed up a pasture hill.

Suddenly, they halted and began whispering to each other. After a minute, Drury explained the situation.

"We're going to listen here for a bird that's roosted in that corner of the woods a lot," he said. "Every time he's been there, he's flown down into that pasture. So if he's there this morning, we're going to slip in, be quiet, and kill him as soon as we can." It sounded logical. I stood and strained my ears to hear the morning's first redbirds.

But almost before Drury had finished talking, a throaty gobble shattered the morning. Drury and Kilmer nearly jumped in the air and then pointed at each other in excitement. That was their bird. And he was right where they wanted him.

Ducking low, we slipped up the field edge to a fence line where the woods met the pasture. The bird was probably 60 steps down the fence line from us, and he and a running buddy were gobbling their heads off by the time we sat down. Drury quickly placed a jake decoy in the pasture and ran back to our setup.

"He's gonna pitch down right into the field, so be ready before fly-down," he said. "I'll have the camera rolling, and I'll give you a signal. But just kill him when you can. Don't let him get away!"

My chest was thumping as I leveled Drury's 11-87 over my knee and pulled up my facemask. The bird was gobbling up a storm, and I couldn't wait to see him touch down.

I didn't wait long. After about twenty minutes, the gobbler clammed up briefly. Soon, a hen landed in the field just below a small rise about 60 yards away. Seconds later, two gobblers sailed silently to her side.

"There he is," Mark whispered from behind me.

When the author shot his then-largest Eastern bird, the calling strategy was simple: Be quiet!

I tried to control my breathing as the lead gobbler strutted for the hen, which did her best to ignore him. The other bird alternately watched his buddy and the hen.

Slowly, the birds began to drift closer and into the center of the pasture. The gobblers saw the jake decoy and eyed it suspiciously. They didn't charge it aggressively, but their body language indicated they weren't happy that a young interloper was in their pasture with their girlfriend. Cautiously and suspiciously, they began walking toward the decoy.

After a few steps, however, they stopped, and the lead bird raised his head. The hen was quartering away from us, and the big gobbler wasn't going to leave her just to beat up some jake. He stood for a minute and then periscoped his head.

It was time. Mark clucked once on his diaphragm call, and I centered the cross-hairs of his scope on the bird and fired. The longbeard crashed down, and the hen and other gobbler got out of town.

I ran to the turkey, more out of excitement than from a need to capture the bird. The load of 3 1/2 -inch No. 5 shot had cleaned his clock, and death had been swift.

Kilmer quickly joined me beside the turkey, elated that he'd finally caught the corner gobbler in a vulnerable spot. We high-fived by the bird and then reached down to grab its legs.

"Holy smokes!" I said, forgetting that Mark had the camera rolling. "Look at these spurs!"

The bird sported genuine 1 1/2 -inch razors. He was by far the biggest-spurred turkey I'd killed at that time. And honestly, it was one of the most exciting hunts I'd ever experienced, even though we'd only uttered one call—a soft cluck when I shot—to the turkey.

No fancy calling or super-secret technique killed that big-spurred gobbler. Rather, the scouting, woodsmanship, and savvy of Drury and Kilmer came through. And even a multiple world champion caller like Mark would take that any day in the turkey woods.

CHAPTER 5

If you know which tree he's in, you can likely make an educated guess about where the turkey will fly down. Remember, in hilly country, birds will almost always pitch down to the short side of the terrain.

TES RANDLE JOLLY

Off the Roost:
Early Morning Strategies

Nothing epitomizes spring turkey hunting like hearing an old gobbler hammer from the roost in the pre-dawn. It's one of the most primordial, spine-tingling experiences in the outdoors.

You slip through the pitch-black woods, trying to stay quiet and mentally running through your game plan. If you roosted a bird the previous night, you know where you're headed. You just want to get there undetected. If you didn't locate one the evening before, you're likely walking to a good listening spot or traditional roosting area.

Either way, when you reach your destination, you stop, calm your nerves, and listen intently for that telltale sound. Sometimes, it happens immediately. Other mornings, you wait for what seems like forever, worried that the sun is rising fast in the east and that you've messed up something.

But when it hits you, it's almost like you've never heard it before. The cool rush of morning breeze and soft musings of cardinals are suddenly shattered by "gggaaaaaaaaaaarrrrrrrrrrobbbbbbbble!"

There he is. You search the gray treetops for a visual, but the sound seems to emanate from the woods itself.

"Gggggggaaaaaaaaaarrrrrrrobbbbbbbble!"

As your fingers tremble, you gently touch your striker to the call, trying to eke out the softest tree-yelp possible. Then you pause; did he hear it?

"Gggggggggaaarrrrrrrobbbbble!"

Indeed. And the spring game begins again. Win or lose—and you'll usually lose, but savor the experience anyway—there's nothing like it.

STARTING OUT

The roost game plays out every spring morning across the country, but it's slightly different in areas with high hunting pressure. Basically, you need to find a bird that won't be bumped, called to, or otherwise goofed up by another hunter. Again, your scouting forays should have provided clues about human activity in your hunting area, and you'll likely have a good idea about easily accessible places that will attract crowds. Still, you must keep the human factor in mind that first morning.

I won't dwell on this, but it bears mention: no matter how tight you roosted a bird or how good your plan is, you should abandon it if you have company. Closely sharing the woods with other turkey hunters—though they're likely safe, conscientious guys just like you—doesn't work. It's unsafe—especially in the dark—and your odds of killing a turkey decrease geometrically.

If you pull up to a parking area and find another truck there, move on. If you camp under a tree but hear another hunter calling nearby at dawn, back out and go elsewhere. If a tom gobbles but you hear a truck pulling off the nearest road, get out. You can always come back later—a great pressured-turkey tactic we'll discuss in the next chapter. Be antisocial, and do your darnedest to find a turkey—or at least a good-looking area—you'll have to yourself.

This is difficult sometimes. If you've scouted a hot gobbler for a week but some dude stumbles in on you the first morning, you certainly won't want to leave the bird for him to booger or kill. But I'm telling you, it's better that way. Odds are he won't kill the turkey, and then you can come back and work the bird later.

Years ago, a fellow writer accepted a Pennsylvania hunt from two pretty well-known callmakers. The first morning, the trio set out on public land and got pretty tight to a hot longbeard. As the sky brightened, however, it became apparent that they weren't alone. In fact, they heard up to five other people in the woods nearby, all calling to the longbeard.

When the gobbler pitched out of the tree, other hunters shot at him twice in the air. Needless to say, he hit the ground running and never made another peep. My friend turned to the callmakers and said, "I cannot do this." With that, he walked out of the woods.

He meant no offense, of course. The callmakers likely hadn't known about their competition before that morning. Still, my friend made it clear that he'd rather hear and see nothing while hunting safely than compete with other folks for even a pepper-hot turkey. That's good advice. Enough said.

Often, you'll only be able to get within 100 yards or so of a roosted turkey, but that's okay. You're still close—likely well within his comfort zone and certainly close enough to work him effectively.

GETTING TIGHT

Now, let's assume you've dodged the hordes and have a patch of woods to yourself. If you roosted a longbeard the previous evening, you probably have a solid plan. Of course, the specifics depend on how precisely you roosted him.

If you know which tree he's in, you can likely make an educated guess about where the turkey will fly down. Remember, in hilly country, birds will almost always pitch down to the short side of the terrain. That is, a gobbler roosted on a sloping ridge will fly to the high side of the ridge—the shortest distance between the tree and the ground—rather than sailing downhill.

In flat country, the equation is a bit more difficult. Birds might just pump their wings and hit the ground right below their tree. Or, they could lock up and sail several hundred yards into a long field or an open area along a ridge. If it's windy, they'll often fly into the wind, just like incoming waterfowl or an airplane that's landing.

One thing is certain: they want to fly down to a safe area, one they can see well from their perch. Usually, such an area is relatively open and offers good visibility, whether it's a 500-acre stubble field or a 10-square-yard opening in the timber directly below the roost tree. Often, turkeys fly down to the same spot from which they flew up to roost the previous evening. After all, it was safe and convenient then, and unless something spooked them during the night, things won't have changed.

When you get a good idea about where a turkey might hit the ground, try to determine the closest viable setup. Do you want to be right at the spot where he'll fly down? Of course not. You'll never get there without bumping him off the roost. A best-case scenario would be setting up within shotgun range of where a gobbler will land. In open woods, field edges, or other cover-challenged areas, that can be difficult. However, in hilly terrain or spots with good cover, you can sometimes do it. For example, in areas such as Missouri, Iowa, or southwestern Wisconsin, turkeys often roost just below ridgetops and then fly down to the high sides of ridges. By sneaking in along ridgelines, you can often be within 50 steps of where gobblers hit the ground.

Just make sure you leave plenty of time to sneak into an area, and prepare to be in the woods when it's pitch black. And if you have any doubts, back off, and play it safe. Remember what Brad Harris said when asked, "How close is too close with a turkey?" One step. And when in doubt, be conservative. If you miss by 10 yards, it probably won't affect your hunt that much. If you take one step too many and spook a gobbler off the roost, your hunt is finished. Often, you'll only be able to get within 100 yards or so of a roosted turkey, but that's okay. You're still close—likely well within his comfort zone and certainly close enough to work him effectively.

Try to find what I call "the ideal setup." Basically, these are areas where you cannot see the turkey—and vice versa—until he is in range. TES RANDLE JOLLY

If you can't set up super tight, try to envision or predict where a turkey will fly down and then how he might work to your calling. Make it easy for the turkey to reach you. For example, if you're pretty certain a turkey will fly down along a logging road high on a ridge, try to choose a setup to which the bird can easily travel. That might be on that logging road farther along the ridge or just above the road on the ridgetop. The principle remains the same: determine an easy, convenient travel route the bird can take from Point A (where he lands) to Point B (where you'll shoot him). It goes without saying that you should avoid calling obstructions, such as creeks, gullies, fences, thick clearcuts, or other potential hangup spots. Your scouting should have revealed these.

Also—and we'll touch more on this later—try to find what I call "the ideal setup." Basically, these are areas where you cannot see the turkey—and vice versa—until he is in range. Whether you're obscured by a slight terrain rise, a patch of gooseberry brush, a bend in a logging road, or a similar scenario, you want to remain hidden from a gobbler. Why? If he looks 100 yards through open woods for the hen he hears calling but can't see her, he knows something is wrong and won't come in. However, if he looks for that hen—and believe me, he knows exactly where you are—but sees nothing, it's natural because the terrain or obstruction is blocking his view. He'll likely approach to see the hen, and he'll usually stop and raise his head for a look the second he clears the terrain rise or obstruction. By that time, you should be sending a swarm of shot toward his noggin.

GETTING SEMI-TIGHT

Roosting a bird the night before you hunt is ideal. However, it's not always possible. Work schedules, travel distance, bad weather, responsibilities at home, or just uncooperative turkeys often foil your best intentions to pinpoint a gobbler. When that happens, don't fret. Provided you scouted hard and learned all you could about the turkeys in your hunting area, you won't be starting completely blind.

Basically, you have two options. First, you can start the morning at a good listening area—a long, open ridge or a high, sprawling vista, for example—hoping to hear gobblers sound off. Then, you can go to them.

This is a great way to hear several turkeys, and you can then hunt the closest or hottest bird. The drawback is obvious: you're likely to be relatively far from the roosted birds, and the fly-down clock will be ticking as you approach them. Often, you can't get as close as you could had you roosted birds the previous night.

There might be another problem, albeit a good one: if you hear several turkeys gobble before dawn, which one should you hunt? As a general

If you hear several turkeys gobble before dawn, which one should you hunt? As a general rule, don't start hot-footing it toward the first longbeard that hammers. Wait until the bird gobbles a few more times. Often, another bird—perhaps closer, hotter, or in a better calling position—will start gobbling, giving you a more ideal option. TES RANDLE JOLLY

rule, don't start hot-footing it toward the first longbeard that hammers. Wait until the bird gobbles a few more times. Often, another bird—perhaps closer, hotter, or in a better calling position—will start gobbling, giving you a more ideal option.

That provides a good general philosophy, too. Which bird should you work? The one that offers the best chance of success. If there's a hot gobbler 100 steps away, slip in a bit closer, and go to work. If a more distant bird is tearing it up, it's probably wise to try him. Of if you hear a bird at an area with which you're very familiar—the proverbial end of that long, timbered point, for example—go to him. It's always a guessing game, but you must weigh several factors—distance, how hot the turkey is, and how good your potential calling setup is—before deciding. Just do it quickly. Remember, daylight is burning.

Your second "blind" option is a bit of a gamble. Start the morning at areas where turkeys have roosted before or spots where turkeys congregate frequently. For example, if you've seen gobblers roost a time or two on a long timbered point in a deep draw, it might be worthwhile to start there in hopes longbeards are nearby. Or, if birds always seem to end up in a bottomland cornfield an hour or two after fly-down, you can set up a portable blind and wait them out. Obviously, scouting plays a big role in these decisions.

When listening for turkeys at dawn, many folks like to use locator calls to elicit a shock-gobble. That's a great option, provided you don't overdo it. Ideally, I like to wait and see if turkeys will gobble on their own. That way, I don't have to disturb the woods one iota as they reveal their location. But some mornings, they're reluctant to gobble, so I might float out one owl-hoot note—a long "whoo-ooh" before dawn. If nothing responds, I'll try two or three more times but then shut up. As the sky brightens, I'll usually switch to a crow call, hawk screamer, or, if I'm trying to throw sound a long way, a coyote howler. Again, if nothing responds after a time or two, I'll put these calls in my pocket. Here's why.

When turkeys shock-gobble, they're not really reacting to the specific sound (it's not like they're mad at owls or crows). They're just natural noises. Turkeys also gobble at airplanes, trucks on a highway, and even gunshots. Someone once described shock-gobbling like this: imagine startling a nervous guy who's had too much caffeine. He'll likely jump or exclaim something. A spring gobbler is so fired up to breed that he's bursting with energy. When you startle him, it's almost as if the gobble slips out in reaction. But the more you use a specific call, the less it startles a turkey and the less effective it becomes.

Your second "blind" option is a bit of a gamble. Start the morning at areas where turkeys have roosted before or spots where turkeys congregate frequently.

One final note: when trying to locate turkeys at dawn, it's important to keep safety and solitude in mind. When you hear a turkey hammer from a distant ridge, it's easy to think solely about slipping up the ridge and finding a setup. But you must also look and listen for like-minded turkey hunters doing the same thing. If you suddenly find you have company, let your competition win that battle, and find another turkey to chase.

LET THE CALLING BEGIN

Guides and outfitters across the country often disagree about the Number One mistake most turkey hunters make. For some, the biggest gaffe is not taking the first good shot, and that's undoubtedly true. However, I'd have to go with the other option: overcalling to roosted birds.

And before you think I'm casting stones, let me assure you I'm not without sin. I've often overcalled—and probably still overcall—to roosted birds. It's just so easy to do. Remember, a longbeard does most of his gobbling from the limb at dawn, and turkey hunters live for that sound. When they yelp and a tom bellows back, it's like feeding an addiction— and it's damn difficult to stop. But by continuing, many turkey hunters seal their fates.

Conservative usually wins the day with roosted gobblers. I only want a gobbler to honor my calling once, and that's all I need to do until the bird is on the ground. As dawn breaks and birds start gobbling, I'll issue one or two soft tree-yelps. If a gobbler answers, I put my call down and wait for fly-down. The bird knows where I am, and he's probably interested. Calling further will only make him hang up on the limb, expecting the hen to come to him. (Sometimes, old or pressured birds remain on the limb for long periods, anyway. Often, they don't fly down until they see hens below them.)

If a gobbler doesn't respond to my calling, I'll wait a couple of minutes and then try another soft tree-cluck or brief series of tree-yelps. If he answers then, great. I put the call away and await fly-down. If not, I'll typically stop calling anyway. Make no mistake: the bird heard you and knows where "the hen" is. He might be roosted near real hens or is just playing hard to get. Either way, further tree-yelping won't help the situation.

There is an exception. As the woods awakens, you'll likely know whether a gobbler is alone or roosted with hens. If he's with ladies, you can probably throw the conservative calling out the window. The old boy will fly down with his harem and follow them to the ends of the earth.

Conservative usually wins the day with roosted gobblers. I only want a gobbler to honor my calling once, and that's all I need to do until the bird is on the ground. As dawn breaks and birds start gobbling, I'll issue one or two soft tree-yelps. If a gobbler answers, I put my call down and wait for fly-down.

Try cranking up your calling with some fly-down cackles and excited yelping and cutting. Make the gobbler think you're the first hen on the ground, and that you're hot to trot. If you're lucky—and you'll have to be, because this doesn't work that often—a bird might pitch down early and try to find that hot hen.

If that isn't your style—and in a heavily hunted area, you might not want to call too much or get a longbeard gobbling like crazy for fear of attracting other hunters—you'll have to wait. Every now and then, a longbeard will fly down away from his hens, and if you're in the right spot, you might cluck-and-purr him close for a quick look (and shot!).

Whether a gobbler responds, keeps quiet, has hens, or is alone, the most critical moment of your fly-down hunt occurs when the big boy sails from his tree to the ground. That's when the true hunt commences.

Usually, even a hot longbeard will gobble less frequently or stop altogether moments before sailing off his roost. Further, because the roost-gobbling period typically lasts fifteen to thirty minutes, you can almost anticipate fly-down. If a bird that's been hammering for twenty-five minutes suddenly goes mute, he's probably preparing to set his wings.

If you're close, you'll often hear the bird—sometimes see him— fly down. You might hear a gobbler pump his wings or make out the

If you're close, you'll often hear the bird—sometimes see him—fly down. You might hear a gobbler pump his wings or make out the snapping of branches or leaves as the bird sails earthward. And many times, you'll hear a dull thump when twenty-some pounds of poultry hits the dirt.

snapping of branches or leaves as the bird sails earthward. And many times, you'll hear a dull thump when twenty-some pounds of poultry hits the dirt.

Other times—often when you're 100 yards or farther from a tom—you won't hear him fly down. One minute, he'll gobble on the limb. The next minute, you'll hear a muffled gobble 50 steps away from the tree. The key is identifying that the bird is on the ground. After you know that, you can implement your calling and maneuvering strategy. Again, the specific approach will depend on whether he's with hens.

If a gobbler doesn't have hens, start him with soft stuff: gentle clucking and purring, and maybe some quiet yelps. Do just enough to sound like a hen that's flown down and is feeding nearby. If the gobbler responds—whether by gobbling or moving closer, or both—stick with that. If he'll work to soft calling, let him do it—especially if he's close.

Lonely gobblers sometimes run in, but that's usually not the case. Often, they seem to strut in place for long, drawn-out minutes—sometimes just out of sight—waiting for the hen to come to them. This seems to be especially true with birds in pressured areas. During these standoffs, you'll be tempted to move on the bird or call more aggressively. Don't. If the tom is responding to your calling and isn't going away, he's interested. He's just playing hard to get. Chances are, he'll eventually be hot or curious enough to look for that hen. If you move on him—whether trying to bushwhack him or slip around him—you might bump him. And if you call too much, you're simply telling the longbeard that the hen is fired up and will be there soon. Also, you'll probably make him gobble more, which might attract hens or human company.

Patience pays big dividends. Remember the words of turkey hunting's poet laureate, Tom Kelly: "You have to pay for every bird you kill, and the coin you use to pay for them is time." If a hot bird hangs up, try scratching in the leaves like a hen scratching for food. Or call and then shut up for ten minutes or more. Often that will play on a gobbler's curiosity and make him break.

Of course, even lonely longbeards can be obstinate and unpredictable, leaving you to ponder whether to sit tight or move. We'll cover this more in the chapter on working turkeys, but I have a general guideline I follow for roost hunts. Unless you know for certain a turkey has picked up hens or is moving away, I'll stick with my setup. Even if a bird goes quiet, I'll stay there at least twenty minutes, hoping to catch him slipping in silently. Moving then would do me no good, anyway. After all, I don't know where the bird went! If I get a fix on his location or travel route, then I'll make a move—but only then.

Patience pays big dividends. Remember the words of turkey hunting's poet laureate, Tom Kelly: "You have to pay for every bird you kill, and the coin you use to pay for them is time."

You can try to lure a longbeard away from hens. I've seen it work, though not often and probably not at all in pressured areas. However, by calling hard at a breeding flock and getting responses from hens and gobblers, you might lure silent satellite longbeards in through the back door.

JENNIFER WEST

If a turkey is roosted with hens, the game changes. He'll hit the ground, puff up like a balloon, and start drumming love tunes at his girls. Oh, sure, he might gobble at your calling, but he's probably not coming. He'll follow the ladies. If you know where the ladies and their man are going, your decision is simple. Get up, try to circle around the birds and ambush them along their travel route. If they drift away on a logging road or long ridge, for example, you can be reasonably sure they'll stay on that path—especially if it leads to a field, food plot, timbered flat, or a larger ridge. Make your decision, execute your move, and carefully, quietly move in front of them and wait. Above all, don't bump the birds, and make sure to get ahead of them. Don't try to fall in behind a moving flock and think you'll yelp them in. That's a sucker bet.

Some folks advocate calling to hens in an attempt to lure them in, along with the gobbler. This works sometimes, but it's probably overrated. In my experience, it works best early in the season, when hens are still sorting out their pecking order and aren't yet serious about breeding. Cutting and aggressive yelping can often drive a boss hen crazy, sending her searching for the intruder. However, when hens get serious about breeding, a cluck or yelp from another hen—you, in this case—can make them trot the other way. They don't want to share their gobbler with some hussie, so they simply drag him away. Later in the season, when hens are nesting, you can get them fired up by calling near their nests. A hen might get agitated and start cutting, prompting a nearby gobbler to sound off or work in. But again, this won't work that often.

You can also try to lure a longbeard away from hens. I've seen it work, though not often and probably not at all in pressured areas. However, by calling hard at a breeding flock and getting responses from hens and gobblers, you might lure silent satellite longbeards in through the back door. Always be prepared for these sneaky subordinate birds.

If you play your roost cards right, you can hoist a longbeard over your shoulder and beat your fellow turkey hunters to the local diner. But many days, through no fault of yours, roost hunts go sour, and you're left looking at the hot sun, wondering what to do next.

Notes from the Turkey Woods

A Fool and his Gobbler

The moral of this story is about as subtle as a freight train. Still, I repeat it often because it's a great example of how to screw up a roost hunt.

Years ago, when I had fewer than five turkey seasons—and maybe three turkeys—under my belt, I heard a longbeard gobble from an isolated patch of timber. My turkey hunting mentors would have told me I needed to cut the distance as much as possible before calling to the bird, so I did. I slipped through the woods, ducked across a marsh cornfield, slipped up a fence line, and settled in by an old oak 80 steps from the bird.

The gobbler was in a huge weeping willow tree bordered by marsh on one side and the small woods on the other. He hadn't seen me, and he was hot as a jalapeño pepper.

Nervously, I popped my diaphragm call in my mouth and did my best rendition of a yelp. Between you and me, it stunk, but the turkey liked it. He shot a machine-gun gobble back at me, and then followed it up with a double-gobble.

Holy smokes! I was really turkey hunting.

The bird was alone, and he had fallen all over my calling. My heart pounded like a triphammer at the thought of yelping in and killing that swamp turkey.

In hindsight, the trap was obvious, yet I fell for it like a buck fawn hitting a corn pile. If one series of yelps had fired him up, another—and then some more—would drive him crazy and make him run to my shotgun barrel.

So I yelped again, and the turkey gobbled. I clucked, and the turkey gobbled. I stopped briefly to catch my breath, and the turkey gobbled. Not wanting to lose steam—and trying to get my money's worth from those Real Turkeys practice tapes—I yelped some more. Yep. The turkey gobbled.

Looking back, I realize that bird probably would have gobbled at an air horn or a Metallica CD, but I didn't know that then. By God, I was going to yelp that longbeard in and tell everyone at the office about it.

But soon, something seemed amiss, even to my naive idea of turkey hunting. The bird was still hot, but he'd been in the tree an awfully long time. Further, after thirty-some minutes, the marsh was illuminated in bright sunlight, so the bird could pretty much see everything around him. But being stubborn and stupid, I continued blowing my call.

You can guess what happened next. The bird eventually pitched out of the tree and rubber-necked away through the small woods. He'd hung up on the limb for forty or more minutes, certain that loud-mouthed hen would work her way to

Looking back, I realize that bird probably would have gobbled at an air horn or a Metallica CD, but I didn't know that then. By God, I was going to yelp that longbeard in and tell everyone at the office about it.

him. And when the sun rose, revealing nothing but corn stalks and a funny-looking blob along the fence line, he'd seen enough and decided he had important business elsewhere.

A decoy might have helped, but I still would have called way too much and hung the bird up in the tree, thereby blowing the hunt. I never saw that turkey again. I suspect the neighbor might have killed him that season, though I can't confirm it. Still, years later, that marsh gobbler remains with me. Every time a longbeard gobbles from the roost and I prepare to call, I think of the longbeard and the painful lesson he imparted.

Oh, don't get me wrong. I still want to yelp and hear a roosted bird gobble. Let's just say I've been shamed into silence.

CHAPTER 6

Even if turkeys aren't gobbling their heads off at midday, you're still in the game. Early in the season, when gobblers are fired up but hens aren't yet serious about breeding, you're apt to elicit a response from a longbeard at any time.

Up in the Day

I'll always remember how excited I was in 1997 when I hunted with Mark Drury for the first time. He was a world-champion caller, the hottest name in call-making and, from all reports, a flat-out turkey killing machine. I could only imagine the exclusive estate we'd be privileged to hunt.

And sure enough, the first day was like a dream. A coworker killed a big gobbler while hunting with world-champion caller Don Shipp, and I scored at noon while hunting a gorgeous farm with world champ Steve Stoltz. Man, it was like fantasy camp for turkey hunters.

So imagine my surprise at midmorning the second day of our hunt when Drury pulled up to . . . a small state wildlife area!

"He must not like me," I thought. "What did I say that offended him?"

As it turned out, nothing. I quickly learned that Drury and his crew—who are indeed privileged to hunt some fabulous private areas—routinely hunted and killed turkeys during mid- and late-morning hunts at heavily pressured public hunting areas.

That floored me. This turkey-industry giant was traipsing spots any average Joe could hunt, but he said it made perfect sense.

"There are a lot of birds there," he said nonchalantly. And although I never killed a turkey in those areas with Mark, we had numerous close encounters and quality mid- to late-morning hunts.

Mid- and late morning—"up in the day," as they say down South—are when hunters in pressured areas can really make hay. Much of your competition will have vanished as guys leave for work or family obligations, or just because birds have gone silent. Further, the turkeys you heard at dawn didn't go anywhere, and your chances of catching a lonely gobbler without hens increases as morning wears on.

The woods are quiet, and the sun beats hot on the woods. But look around you: the hordes have thinned out, leaving you to chase turkeys in relative solitude. Make the most of it.

And although the early-morning roost hunt epitomizes turkey hunting, I'd honestly rather hunt later in the morning. I've killed more gobblers from 9 A.M. to 1 P.M. than I have right out of the tree, and many other experienced turkey hunters will tell you the same thing. You might burn some shoe leather, and you probably won't hear as much gobbling as you did at fly-down, but your odds of seriously working a bird are damn good.

THE QUIET TIME

As mentioned, many folks leave the woods by 7 or 8 A.M. It's easy to understand why. Often, especially during the peak of the breeding season, gobblers fly down with hens or quickly find girlfriends, and then zip their beaks. The woods, which once seemed so alive with gobbling and hen talk, might be as quiet as a soundproof chamber. After all, if gobblers are with hens, they don't have much cause to sound off. Oh, they'll spit and drum for their ladies and might offer a courtesy gobble at calling or loud noises, but that's about it. And even if gobblers aren't with hens, they just don't gobble much some days—especially in hard-hunted areas.

Many folks take this silence as a sign that their hunt is finished. "The birds aren't talking," some say. "They're henned up and quiet," others say. "It might be better tomorrow."

True enough. But again, the turkeys are still there, and even if they're not gobbling their heads off, you're still in the game. Early in the season, when gobblers are fired up but hens aren't yet serious about breeding, you're apt to elicit a response from a longbeard at any time. During the two- or three-week peak breeding time—the toughest period to hunt— you can still find lonely toms when hens slip away to lay an egg. And when hens start sitting on their nests, you'll often find lonely solo gobblers seeking companionship during mid- and late morning.

Sure, the early-morning frenzy is done. Yeah, the woods are quiet, and the sun beats hot on the woods. But look around you: the hordes have thinned out, leaving you to chase turkeys in relative solitude. Make the most of it. Usually, hunters fall into one of two midday-tactic camps: passive or aggressive. Both work, but there's a time and place for each.

THE AGGRESSIVE MIDDAY METHOD

Whether you call it walking and calling or cutting and running, this tactic is very popular nowadays, and for good reason: it's fun, it's active, and in the right situations, it's extremely effective. It lets you cover lots of ground and call to multiple turkeys.

This is by far my favorite hunting method—to a fault. Years ago, I pretty much walked and called exclusively during midday. I knew patience and planning killed turkeys, but I wanted to walk and call, so I did. I've tempered that approach somewhat the past few years, and my

Whether you call it walking and calling or cutting and running, this tactic is very popular nowadays, and for good reason: it's fun, it's active, and in the right situations, it's extremely effective.

success rate has increased. That's not a knock on aggressive hunting. It just means you must use your head and choose the method most appropriate to the situation. Given a choice, I'll still take cutting and running over any other tactic. I'm just not stubborn about it.

Basically, cutting and running works best if you have access to large, contiguous tracts of land with sufficient cover—whether it's timber, uneven terrain, or something else—to conceal your movement. It also works well if you have access to several smaller properties, which you can prospect from the road or via quick walks.

If you hunt open areas—flat prairies, rolling pastures, or expansive, sparsely wooded flats, for example—it doesn't work as well because turkeys are much more likely to see you and spook. That also holds true early in the season, when the open woods can make you stick out like a sore thumb.

Cutting and running also doesn't work so well if birds aren't responding well to calling. This is a fine line. It only takes one gobble to turn a bad cut-and-run hunt into a smash hit. Conversely, it only takes one step over ridge—after hearing nothing for an hour—to send a gobbler scurrying for cover. How do you discern between a tough-yet-viable hunt and a hopeless situation? Shoot, when you figure that out, let me know. Generally,

Basically, cutting and running works best if you have access to large, contiguous tracts of land with sufficient cover—whether it's timber, uneven terrain, or something else— to conceal your movement.

you have to judge the mood of the birds. If you're hearing a gobble now and then—in response to your calling or unsolicited—you probably have a decent chance of locating a bird when cutting and running. If turkeys have been sealed up tighter than a drum for two or three days, you're likely better off going with a more passive approach. Of course, rain, wind, hot weather, or intense pressure can make gobblers clam up, too, so those conditions can also make for tough cutting-and-running conditions.

Finally, and perhaps most important, cutting and running often doesn't work as well with pressured turkeys. Maybe that's because pressured birds often seem to work to calling more cautiously—and sometimes silently—than their unpressured cousins. Or perhaps pressured turkeys have been bumped by other cutt-and-run hunters and are not eager to repeat that experience. Either way, in my experience, the aggressive method isn't quite as magical with hard-hunted birds.

However, it still works in many cases. Remember my public-land hunts with Drury? I can assure you he did not sit by an oak for two hours uttering a soft cluck here and there. No, he hit those properties with a head-first run-and-gun attack, often driving from spot to spot, calling aggressively from the road and only hoofing into the woods if a bird responded. You'll be sick of hearing this by the time you've finished this book, but pressured turkeys are still turkeys. They still want to breed hens, and if you catch them in the right mood, they'll gobble and come to calling. So, if you can run and gun for pressured turkeys, do it. Just tweak your approach slightly.

Usually cutting and running means walking and calling. Traipse along ridgelines, field edges, logging roads, or other terrain, moving slowly and quietly, taking care not to be "skylighted" in hilly spots. Stop at least every 100 yards to call—more if you find likely spots. Use box and friction calls—they're louder and usually carry farther—to cast yelps, clucks, and cutting into hollows, off ridges, or across fields, hoping to get a response from a lonely gobbler.

Here are two cutt-and-run calling tips: first, never call unless you have a viable setup nearby. If you yelp and a bird hammers back from 50 steps, you can't take 30 seconds to find the ideal position. You need to grab a tree. Identify good setup spots before you call. That way, if a gobbler is close, you're ready to sit, level your gun across your knee, and kill him.

Along with that, try to identify good setups as you walk. Remember my ideal setup, in which you can't see an incoming bird until he's in range? Keep an eye out for those as you walk logging roads or approach terrain rises. If you spot a likely setup, stop and call from there. If a bird answers, man, you're in business.

Never call unless you have a viable setup nearby. If you yelp and a bird hammers back from 50 steps, you can't take 30 seconds to find the ideal position. You need to grab a tree.

When running and gunning, it's best to start with soft calling and, if necessary, work your way up. Remember, you can't take back aggressive calling. You never know if a bird might be close, and starting a sequence with ultra-loud cutting might do more harm than good if Mr. Gobbler is 60 steps away.

Usually I'll run through three calling sequences each time I stop. First, I'll cluck and yelp softly and then wait for a response. Then, I might yelp louder and throw in some cutting. Finally, I'll end with fairly loud yelping, some aggressive cutting, or both. If nothing answers, I'll move on. Hint: keep your sequences fairly brief. A twenty-note burst of cutting might sound pretty, but if a gobbler hammers during note number three, you probably won't hear it.

Further, mix up your calls. Don't just hammer one glass call for an entire ridge or calling sequence. Start with a friction, go to a box, and finish with a mouth call, or vice versa. Mix it up. Often, turkeys hone in on one specific sound and might react only to that.

Using Drury's twist on running and gunning, you can drive from spot to spot and prospect from the road or parking areas. Driving really lets you cover territory without wasting valuable time. Whether you're walking or driving, it's important to remember the Rule of Three when running and gunning. That is, it's usually wise to make a bird gobble three times before you go to him. Often, turkeys will give a "courtesy gobble" when they hear a new call. Perhaps they think this is a new hen in their area, or maybe the fresh sound stimulates them. Either way, they'll sometimes respond once as if to say, "Come join us!" Then, they often clam up. Usually, courtesy gobbles come from birds with hens. Or sometimes, a gobbler might have drifted 50 or 60 yards from his hens, and when the ladies hear him respond to calling, they get jealous and come back to him.

So if you call once and a turkey gobbles, great. But call again to see if he'll respond a second time. If he does, that's a good sign. Still, try a third sequence, ideally incorporating soft yelps. If he responds to that, you can be fairly certain he wasn't courtesy- or shock-gobbling, and you're likely in the hunt.

There are two important exceptions to the Rule of Three. If you call and a bird gobbles 75 yards away, sit down, and get ready. If he's alone, he might run you over. If he's with hens, fine, but you'll quickly determine that from your setup.

Also, if you finally pull a gobble from a turkey during a day or week when nothing else is happening, you might as well try him. After all, he told you where he was. If he's the only game in town, give him a go.

There's another very important consideration when cutting and running. Usually, many of the turkeys that respond will be relatively far away—say 100 yards or farther. Ideally, you'll want to cut the distance before working them. And any time you move on a turkey, things can get tricky.

Sometimes you might be able to slip within 60 or so steps of a bird, which is great. Close counts, and the less distance a gobbler must travel to reach you, the better your odds of killing him. However, don't take risks. If you can safely get within 100 yards but aren't sure about 95, play it safe, and work the bird from there.

If you have a choice, never go directly toward a turkey. Always take a ten- to twenty-degree slant during your approach, preferably staying at the same elevation or higher than the bird. Remember, the turkey has gobbled at your calling, so he might be fired up and could be approaching you. You don't want to meet him halfway.

Unless a bird is gobbling his proverbial head off—it happens sometimes but not often with pressured gobblers—you must keep tabs on his location somehow as you approach. Some guys—including Drury—like to call their way to a turkey. If the bird responds, they keep track of his location while approaching and fire him up. Then, they can set up and go silent, driving the bird wild. Other folks like to use locator calls to elicit shock-gobbles as they approach. This keeps them abreast of the bird's whereabouts but eliminates the risk of calling him in before they're ready. In my experience, Drury's method probably works better, but it's riskier. Go ahead and call your way to that turkey, but just make sure he keeps responding. If he goes silent for a time, sit down, and get ready. He might be coming.

If the scenario is right and turkeys are responsive, these methods will work—even in hard-hunted areas. Still, you might have to temper your run-and-gun hunting somewhat in pressured areas. Here are some tips.

If you strike a turkey but he won't work, wait until he clams up or drifts off. Then, slip as close as possible to his last known location, set up, wait a few minutes, and call softly for an hour or so. Sometimes, old birds just drift back and forth in safe ridges, flats, or openings. If you get in his comfort zone and make like a hen, he might come back for a look.

When you strike a gobbler in a heavily hunted area, try to "get him killed" with as little gobbling as possible. Everyone loves to hear a long-beard hammer, but that wonderful sound attracts company from hens and human predators. If a bird is hot, cut the distance, call once or twice, and then consider shutting up. Make the bird hunt for you. He might still continue to gobble, but you can't control that. Hopefully, he'll approach fairly quickly without attracting too much attention.

THE PASSIVE APPROACH

Let's switch gears and discuss more hands-off midday methods. Low-impact tactics work very well if you hunt small tracts, open areas, or flat terrain. Honestly, considering the modern turkey boom, they're not bad tactics for any scenario. In the old days, cutting and running was often the only choice because turkey populations were relatively low. But now, with record bird numbers across the country, it's a good bet that at least one gobbler can hear your calling 90 to 95 percent of the time at almost any setup. Also, passive hunting works especially well if turkeys are quiet, pressured, or funky because of weather.

Basically, passive turkey hunting means setting up, calling, and being patient (otherwise called cold-calling). Your pre-season scouting should have revealed some areas turkeys frequent, such as a stubble field, an oak-studded ridge, a fertile creek bottom, a bench filled with scratchings, or similar spots. Sneak into a likely spot, find a comfortable setup, let the woods quiet down for a bit, and listen for turkey noises, whether it's distant calling or nearby drumming. You never know.

Generally it's best to start with soft calling, trying to mimic a hen or hens that are feeding or just moving through an area. I'll often issue one or two clucks and then go into some soft clucking and purring.

Low-impact tactics work very well if you hunt small tracts, open areas, or flat terrain. Honestly, considering the modern turkey boom, they're not bad tactics for any scenario.

If someone else hunted a hotspot early in the morning, or you heard a guy work but not kill a gobbler nearby, consider slipping into that area and calling softly for an hour or two.

Many hunters take several favorite calls and lay them in a semicircle around them, or at least where they can be reached. Then they begin calling with one call and slowly work their way around the circle, trying to find a particular sound or pitch that gets a response. Often, birds won't gobble until you're into your second or third trip through the semicircle.

Generally it's best to start with soft calling, trying to mimic a hen or hens that are feeding or just moving through an area. I'll often issue one or two clucks and then go into some soft clucking and purring. Then, I'll wait three or four minutes and try some soft yelps. I'll stick with this slow, easy approach for the better part of an hour. If I don't hear any gobbling, I might call louder and throw in some more aggressive yelps and cutting.

Obviously, this approach requires patience. You should stay at a setup for at least an hour, and if it's a really hot spot—a ridge filled with fresh scratchings, for example—you might consider staying two or three. Odds are, an old longbeard will slip through looking for a hen.

Of course, not every spot will produce every time. That's why it's wise to have several spots—or better, several spots at several properties—to hit during a day. Blinds often work well in such situations. You can slip from calling station to calling station, ease into a blind, spend an hour or two at an area, and then move to the next one.

As mentioned, the passive approach is ideal for pressured birds. By sitting tight, you greatly reduce the chances of encountering other hunters or spooking turkeys while walking. Also, it's a great way to kill birds other guys worked early in the day. If someone else hunted a hotspot early in the morning, or you heard a guy work but not kill a gobbler nearby, consider slipping into that area and calling softly for an hour or two. There's a school of turkey hunting thought that contends a gobbler will eventually stand in your boot tracks at every place you called during a day. That might be an exaggeration, but it illustrates a point: if you know birds are in an area, or heard someone working a turkey at a spot, those longbeards probably didn't drift too far away. Through patience and realistic—in this case, soft and subtle—calling, you might pull a lonely gobbler back for a look.

And as mentioned, weather conditions can often dictate a passive approach. In mist and rain, turkeys often head to open areas, such as clear-cuts or agricultural fields. Many people believe they do this because the rain obscures their vision and hampers their hearing in the woods, so turkeys feel safer in fields. I don't know if that's true, but birds generally hit fields when it's wet. If the forecast calls for a day of rain, it's probably wise to find a comfortable setup or place a blind near a field.

Notice I said "near a field." Don't set up at an oak right on the field edge. Turkeys can easily pick you out. Set up 10 to 20 steps inside the woods. That provides better cover and also hides the source of your calling better. There is an exception to this—one we'll cover further later in the book. If birds are consistently hitting or traveling through a large field, place a portable blind in that area. Unlike deer, turkeys won't view the blind as a threat.

Windy days are worse than rainy days. Generally, turkeys try to get out of heavy wind, so you might find them in creek bottoms, the lee sides of ridges, or similar spots. And because walking and calling is tough during windy days—you'll have trouble hearing turkeys and vice versa—it's often wise to set up in these areas and be patient.

Likewise, when the weather gets hot—say, sunny and warmer than 70 degrees—turkey activity decreases noticeably. Hey, you don't feel too ambitious during hot days, especially if you're wearing black clothing, do you? Neither do turkeys. They'll often loaf in shady wooded areas, such as flats, points, knobs, or benches. Set up in these spots, and plan to spend several hours there. It might be boring, but it's a killer tactic for hot days when nothing else is going on.

There's one more tactic you might try during mid- and late-morning hunts, and it's somewhat of a hybrid between the aggressive and passive methods. Instead of running and gunning, I'll call it piddling and crawling. Basically, it's a very slow, subtle, and meticulous way of walking and calling. Slip into an area, wait a few minutes, and call softly for fifteen to thirty minutes. If nothing happens, slip 50 yards farther and repeat your calling sequence. This is a great way of covering every inch of a small parcel. Further, it incorporates an extremely important and often-overlooked aspect of turkey calling: movement, or at least the illusion of movement. After all, real hens don't often stand still and call for several hours.

Apply the aggressive, passive, or in-between method to your area, and see which works best consistently. You'll soon gain a feel for the best method at specific times, and learning that difference will provide a huge boost to your success rate.

There's one more tactic you might try during mid- and late-morning hunts, and it's somewhat of a hybrid between the aggressive and passive methods. Slip into an area, wait a few minutes, and call softly for fifteen to thirty minutes. If nothing happens, slip 50 yards farther and repeat your calling sequence.

TES RANDLE JOLLY

Notes from the Turkey Woods

The Worst of Turkeys, the Best of Turkeys

It seems like every time you count on a late-morning or afternoon hunt to save the day, it never does. But now and then, God bless 'em, turkeys read and obey the textbook. And thank goodness.

Several years ago, I joined some friends for opening day at The Roost hunting lodge in Alabama's famous Black Belt. The first morning, world-champion caller Don Shipp and I marched to a small ridge overlooking a vast pond and prepared to call. First, however, Shipp eased to the woodline and peered into a field to the east. As he scuttled back quickly, I knew he'd seen something.

"There are two or three gobblers with a wad of hens there," he said. "We can't get any closer, so we'll have to try them here."

I got on my belly and leveled the gun toward a point of woods in front of me. Shipp yelped, and a gobbler responded immediately.

"I think we'll have to shoot this turkey right in front of us," Shipp whispered. "Be ready."

Shipp called again, and before I knew it, a shimmering longbeard rubbernecked into view at 15 steps. I followed the bird with my gun, leveled the bead on the bird's neck and fired.

Even before I had recovered from the recoil, I knew something was wrong.

"Get on him!" Shipp said excitedly.

The shot had flipped the bird over, but the gobbler had jumped up and started running. I jumped to my knees, swung on the bird and fired another round . . . into the dirt five steps behind the longbeard.

"Get on him!" Shipp said again.

Checking to make sure my gun's safety was on, I ran a few steps toward the gobbler, stopped, clicked the safety off and fired again—and missed.

Shipp and I sprinted after the bird for about 100 more yards, but you can guess the outcome. The turkey got away. In hindsight, I had probably just nicked the bird's neck, stunning it, wounding it slightly and scaring the holy crap out of it.

Dejected and embarrassed, I returned to the lodge, knowing I'd blown a golden opportunity at an opening-day Alabama gobbler.

I smiled when other hunters razzed me about the hunt and tried to keep my chin up. Still, when the subject of an afternoon hunt came up, I felt somewhat sheepish. I didn't want to screw up again! But lodge owner George Mayfield insisted I hunt, and friends Larry Shockey and Matt Morrett would accompany me. What choice did I have?

*When the Good Lord gives
you a redemption gobbler
up in the day, you sure
want to take advantage.*
JENNIFER WEST

I wasn't too worried when we stepped out of the truck. It was a warm, breezy Alabama afternoon, the kind of day when turkeys really don't do much. I figured we'd probably walk and call a bit and then try to roost a bird later. But when Shockey's screaming glass call induced a distant gobble minutes later, I knew it would be no lazy afternoon.

We scrambled up a small levee and called again. Ker-pow! Two birds answered, and they were closing fast. Morrett and I ducked into some bottom-land timber while Shockey stayed near a small point of woods and stopped calling. Morrett yelped once on a mouth call, and the birds cut him off. They were approaching, but I hoped they would come to us rather than Shockey.

Seconds later, I saw the duo running through the woods. They stopped once to strut and gobble, and then continued toward us. Within a minute, they were standing 20 steps away, gawking for the hen they'd heard. I dug my cheek into the stock, concentrated ultra-hard on the lead gobbler's neck, begged for mercy, and then squeezed the trigger.

The bird collapsed, and this time, he stayed down. Just to make sure, I raced from my setup and grabbed the gobbler. Smiling, Morrett stood, lowered his facemask, and walked toward me.

"I thought you were going to tackle that turkey," he said, laughing.

Me too. Shoot, when the Good Lord gives you a redemption gobbler up in the day, you sure want to take advantage. ✍

When he finally raced down a small ridge and stood among the oaks 25 steps away, the setting sun shimmered on his black, copper-tinted feathers, and his red-and-white head glowed like a lighthouse in the fog. He might have been the prettiest gobbler I've ever seen.

The Late Shift: Afternoons and Evenings

I've really never been one to name turkeys. Some people like to, but I usually run out of creative monikers by the second or third tough bird I encounter every season. I guess professor-types call that anthropomorphism, and that doesn't sound like a word that can be trusted. Still, I couldn't help myself with Sundown. It was just too perfect.

Sundown was a Rio Grande gobbler that lived near Eldorado, Texas. He answered my yelps on an aluminum call late one April afternoon, and then closed the distance between us in minutes, gobbling his head off all the way. When he finally raced down a small ridge and stood among the live oaks 25 steps away, the setting sun shimmered on his black, copper-tinted feathers, and his red-and-white head glowed like a lighthouse in the fog. He might have been the prettiest gobbler I've ever seen. I'll never forget the sight and sound of that bird, or the lessons he taught me about afternoon gobblers.

THE LATE, LATE SHOW

I'll be the first to admit that afternoon and evening hunting isn't like early morning, late morning, or even midday hunting. Depending on the weather, temperature, and stage of the breeding season, birds are often less active and much less vocal. However, afternoon and evening hunting is still worthwhile—especially when chasing pressured turkeys. Remember, most human hunting pressure occurs during the early morning. By 8 or 9 A.M., most guys have given up, gone to work, or have other business

Afternoon and evening hunting is still worthwhile—especially when chasing pressured turkeys. Remember, most human hunting pressure occurs during the early morning. By 8 or 9 A.M., most guys have given up, gone to work, or have other business to attend to.

to attend to. If you slip into the woods at 2 or 3 P.M., you'll often have them to yourself—even at heavily hunted public areas.

Temperature is often the major factor in the activity level of afternoon birds. If it's sunny and warm, birds won't be prancing around in the heat. Hens likely fed during the cool morning hours, and if they had a mind to breed or lay an egg, they already took care of that, too. But when the mercury rises and the sun is high, hens and gobblers usually seek to escape the heat by loafing in shaded areas. Many times, they even sit or squat to conserve energy.

It's not always 70 degrees and sunny during turkey season, so birds won't loaf every day away. If it's raining or misting, they'll often be in fields or other open areas throughout the day. If it's windy, they'll find a place out of the gale, whether it's the leeward side of ridges or a deep, fertile hollow. And if temperatures are cool or the sky is overcast, birds might be more active throughout the day, especially early in spring.

Several years ago, I joined good friend and expert turkey hunter Scott Bestul for an early-season Minnesota hunt. The first day and a half was a bust, with pouring rain, high winds, and ice on our windshields the second morning. It was more a test of wills than a real turkey hunt.

But as the storm front cleared out of the area about noon the second day, something funny happened. The gobblers got active—big-time. Bestul and I didn't kill a bird that day, but we legitimately worked four longbeards and messed around with another flock, too. We should have killed a bird on an open ridge near a town park, but impatience doomed us. The point is, turkeys don't watch the clock. If conditions are right, they'll feed, gobble, strut, and do other turkey things at 3 P.M. just like they would at 7 A.M. Just because the noon whistle has blown, you cannot assume the birds will go underground. It's still worthwhile to hunt.

Of course, as evening approaches—even during hot days—hens will make another feeding run, and gobblers will follow. Again, depending on temperatures and the phase of the breeding season, it seems like the best action is after 5 P.M. Gobblers will crank up—or, more accurately, can be cranked up—during this time. They usually won't gobble as much as

Temperature is often the major factor in the activity level of afternoon birds. If it's sunny and warm—about 70 degrees seems to be the magic number—birds won't be prancing around in the heat. TES RANDLE JOLLY

they did during the morning, but I've seen some lonely birds gobble their throats hoarse during frenzied evening calling sessions.

As the sun nears the horizon, turkeys will filter back toward roosting areas. They sense the urgency of finding a safe place to spend the night, so although they might respond to your calls, it's often tough to pull birds off their predetermined course immediately before roosting. And by the time the sky dims, they'll be perched in a tree for another night.

GETTING AFTER THEM IN THE AFTERNOON

So, how do you hunt afternoon turkeys? At the risk of being flippant, pretty much the same way you hunt morning and midday birds. The keys are being aware and patient. As with midmorning and midday hunting, you can choose one of two roads: passive or aggressive. But with afternoon hunting, even the aggressive method is much more passive.

In the Deep South, turkey hunters often hunt pretty aggressively during the morning, take a break for lunch, and then sit at a green field or chufa patch during the afternoon and evening. That's not a bad tactic. Basically, you're setting up at a spot turkeys frequent, calling now and then, being patient, and waiting for something to happen. You can apply that mind-set to many other likely afternoon setups, such as promising loafing areas like water sources, shaded ridges, cool creek bottoms, points, or heads with a mixture of hardwoods and pines. If it's raining, glass or set up at open areas. If it's windy, find a calm area.

If you crave action, this type of hunting is not for you. It often involves hour after hour of sitting, listening, and wondering where the birds are. However, when birds aren't active or vocal, walking and calling or otherwise bumbling through the woods often accomplishes nothing but spooking turkeys. And if birds are already pressured, you want to avoid this.

If you can't stand to sit and wait, you might try a modified version of walking and calling. South Carolina turkey hunter David Findley once called this "piddling and crawling." Basically, instead of charging along ridgelines or logging roads and hammering the hills with yelps and cutting, you slip through the woods—almost as if you were still-hunting deer—stop every 50 or so yards, call softly for a few minutes, and then move on. It's just a much slower, low-key version of running and gunning.

Blinds work well with this type of hunting. If you carry a portable blind or have access to some permanent blinds on a property, it isn't a bad idea to slip from area to area, call a bit at each one, and then move on if nothing happens.

One more note: Findley, a huge proponent of afternoon hunting, often says that realism in calling is very important during the late shift. You

Top: *As with midmorning and midday hunting, you can choose one of two roads for afternoons: passive or aggressive. But even the aggressive method is much more passive.*
Right: *In the Deep South, turkey hunters often hunt pretty aggressively during the morning, take a break for lunch, and then sit at a green field or chufa patch during the afternoon and evening. That's not a bad tactic.*

want to sound like a hen would at that time. She'll probably be purring or softly clucking while cruising through the woods. Keep it soft and subtle.

Often, afternoon gobblers simply pop in for a look. You might hear nothing more than shuffling in the leaves or drumming. Remain alert for these sounds at all times. You never know when a lonely longbeard might visit, and you must be ready for the opportunity. If, however, a bird fires up and starts hammering gobbles, play him like you would any other turkey. Take his temperature, and call him to the gun.

WHEN NIGHT COMES DOWN

As evening nears—again, let's say 5 P.M. or later—hunting gets more interesting. Hens will hit the feed bag before heading to the roost, and gobblers will follow. Lonely toms might fire up and try to find some hens to roost with. This window might be brief, but if you hit it right, it's great.

Again, you can follow the passive or aggressive road. Passive evening hunters often hedge their bets by choosing a setup near a likely roosting area. (Not under the roost tree, of course, but near it. Shooting birds at a roost might net you a gobbler, but it does nothing for long-term success in that area.) That way, they're fairly certain birds will be in the area, and if

As evening nears, hunting gets more interesting. Hens will hit the feed bag before heading to the roost, and gobblers will follow. Lonely toms might fire up and try to find some hens to roost with.

You can follow the passive or aggressive road during evenings. Passive evening hunters often hedge their bets by choosing a setup near a likely roosting area. (Not under the roost tree, of course, but near it.)

nothing else, they might see or hear them fly up and gain a leg up for the next morning.

Large fields or ridges near roosting sites are great for this type of hunting. Often hens, with gobblers in tow, will feed across ag fields or along hardwood ridges on their way to roost. If you're there to intercept them or at least get a visual, all the better.

You can call a bit more during evening than afternoon. After all, the temperature is likely decreasing, and birds will be more active. As such, your chances of getting a response from a hot gobbler are far better. Don't get too carried away, but don't be afraid to yelp, cluck, or even cutt every few minutes.

Aggressive evening hunters pretty much get after turkeys like they would at mid- or late morning. You can walk and call through likely areas, especially near roost sites. Be extra careful not to bump or spook birds because that could screw up your morning hunt.

Aggressive evening hunters pretty much get after turkeys like they would at mid- or late morning. You can walk and call through likely areas, especially near roost sites. Be extra careful not to bump or spook birds because that could screw up your morning hunt. JENNIFER WEST

If you strike a bird as the sun is getting low, remember that your window is very brief. Turkeys will draw a line in the sand before fly-up. That is, they might continue gobbling at your calling, but they know roosting time is approaching, and they usually won't come in if it's too late. So, if you hit a hot bird, do your best with him, but know when to say when. If the sun is setting, and he just gobbles in one spot for several minutes, you're probably out of luck. You might consider backing off, pinpointing where he flies up, and trying him again the next day.

Usually, birds that are lonely and hot when they fly up to roost will remain hot the next morning. Usually. That's not always the case. However, if you spy a hot, lonely longbeard one night, you need to get after him the next day. He's probably the best bet in town, and you won't know otherwise unless you try.

LATE, GREAT TURKEYS

Never discount afternoon and evening hunting. A turkey hunter should never give up, knowing that being in the woods is the only way to take advantage of opportunity. And if you're hunting heavily pressured areas, afternoons and evenings might provide a welcome solace from crowded morning hunts. Use your head, adjust your tactics somewhat, and give it your all in the P.M. I promise you'll be surprised.

If you hit a hot bird, do your best with him, but know when to say when. If the sun is setting, and he just gobbles in one spot for several minutes, you're probably out of luck. You might consider backing off, pinpointing where he flies up, and trying him again the next day. TES RANDLE JOLLY

Notes from the Turkey Woods

Eight Pounds of Afternoon Trouble

Some folks say afternoon turkey hunting is a different game. But I promise you, afternoon gobblers are every bit as evil as their morning counterparts.

Years ago, I joined Gary Sefton of Woods Wise Calls at the famed White Oak Plantation near Tuskegee, Alabama. One warm March afternoon, Sefton, guide Joe Smith, and I decided to set up in a pine plantation that overlooked a hardwood swamp. Smith wasn't overly optimistic, but he knew there were birds in the area and promised to give it his best shot. We eased into the pines, found comfortable setups under the green canopy, settled ourselves, and then started calling.

Lo and behold, Sefton's first yelps were met with a throaty gobble from the swamp! And it was no courtesy gobble, either. Soon, the turkey was choking himself by responding to our calls. Unbelievably, it looked as if we'd struck a red-hot bird during a warm afternoon. Perhaps we'd return to the lodge, bird in tow, for cocktails before sundown!

The gobbler played it in classic fashion, gobbling and moving, and steadily approaching all the while. After about ten minutes, it seemed we'd see the bird's snowball head pop up from the swamp at any second. He was close enough that the rattle from his gobble was easily audible.

Then, things got even better. A hen—presumably heading toward a roost area—wandered in behind us and began yelping incessantly. We called over and around her, and the gobbler went berserk. He'd probably run in!

Of course, you can guess the outcome. The hen, God bless her, soon became wary of the "calling trees" she saw, and cut a wide path around us. She could have walked out of the plantation, leaving the gobbler to us. But no, she took a hard right turn, made a beeline for the big boy and, within seconds, hooked up with the still-hidden tom.

Soon, the woods were silent, and the game was finished. I sighed and dropped my striker. Sefton leaned his head back against a pine. Smith just shook his head and chuckled. We had come within seconds of completing a once-in-a-season afternoon hunt to being whipped—yet again—by an eight-pound hen.

Morning, noon, or evening, that's a heartbreaker. !

Never discount afternoon and evening hunting. A turkey hunter should never give up, knowing that being in the woods is the only way to take advantage of opportunity. And if you're hunting heavily pressured areas, afternoons and evenings might provide a welcome solace from crowded morning hunts. PAT REEVE

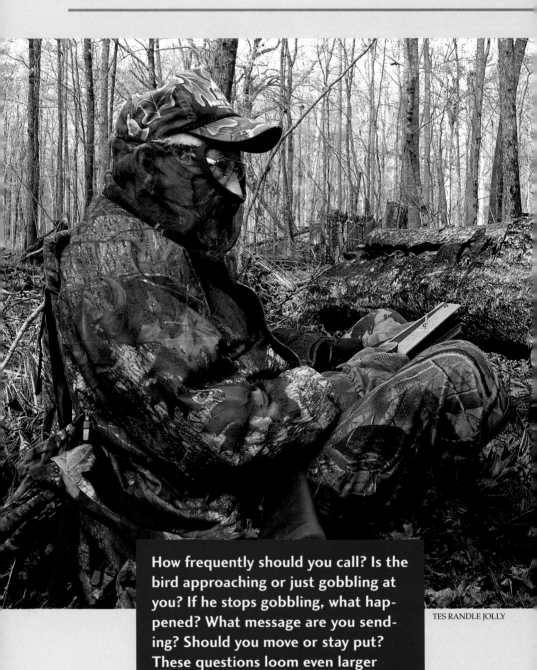

CHAPTER 8

TES RANDLE JOLLY

How frequently should you call? Is the bird approaching or just gobbling at you? If he stops gobbling, what happened? What message are you sending? Should you move or stay put? These questions loom even larger when working pressured turkeys.

The Heat of Battle

Okay, so he was right. Hey, we had a 50–50 shot, and we—all right, I—lost.

Our hunt had started so well. After hearing little before flydown, my friend Dan Barden and I had trekked across a pasture and up a small ridge before stopping to call. At the first cluck, a gobbler hammered back 75 yards away. Barden and I exchanged wide-eyed looks as we scrambled for cover.

The bird was just over a crest in the woods at the field edge, so I anticipated a quick hunt. I yelped softly, and the bird double-gobbled. Man, it was going to be textbook. I switched to soft clucking and purring, scratching occasionally in the leaves. And the turkey gobbled at everything—even on his own. But then, reality set in. After five minutes, the bird hadn't moved. Ditto, ten minutes later.

"Is there a fence down there?" I whispered to Barden.

He nodded.

"We've gotta get on the same side of the fence as him," I said.

Barden shook his head.

"He'll come through it," he said. "There's a low spot where they cross all the time. I've seen them do it for years."

Ten minutes later, though, I wasn't convinced. The bird hadn't moved, and his incessant gobbling would probably soon attract a hen.

"Let's go," I said, standing. Barden eased from his setup and led the way.

We sneaked around the ridge to the north, where a logging road entered the pasture. After ducking through the fence, I kneeled and yelped. The bird hammered back immediately—from the woods, right where we had been five minutes earlier. I bowed my head in disbelief.

"Well, let's sneak back up the logging road and set up," I said.

We did, and the gobbler met us halfway there. We only saw a darting white head and heard a few sharp putts, but the message was clear: "You blew it, chump."

Had I simply stopped calling and stayed put for five minutes, Barden and I would have exchanged high-fives over a flopping gobbler. Instead, I lowered my facemask in shame and cursed. Barden didn't have to say anything. He'd told me so. So it goes when you're in the heat of battle.

During your turkey hunting quests, you'll encounter many similar situations. Your practice, preparation, scouting, game planning, skillful maneuvering, and practical calling will have brought you to the moment of truth: working a turkey. That's when things get interesting.

"Working" a turkey is sort of a misleading term. You know, of course, that it refers to the process of calling in a bird. Sounds simple enough, right? You call, the bird responds, and he comes in . . . in theory. Sometimes, working a bird involves nothing more than clucking once and getting your gun up. Most days, it will be much more involved. And during some hunts, working a turkey will truly be work; a multifaceted effort involving calling, maneuvering, and on-the-spot decision making. If you make the correct decisions, you'll likely experience a hunt to cherish. But if you make one incorrect decision, the encounter will leave you scratch-

First—as always—start with soft calling, even if you're not super-tight to a gobbler. If a turkey responds and reacts to soft, subtle calling, let him. He's probably pepper-hot.

ing your head and doubting your ability. And here's another catch: often, you don't have hard-and-fast guidelines on which to base your decisions.

The process of working a turkey is further complicated by the intensity and excitement of the moment. Calling back and forth with a gobbler, sweating about your next tactic, and anticipating seeing that big boy walking through the woods is exhilarating stuff.

GETTING DOWN TO IT

All right, let's assume you've located a bird, set up, and started calling. Immediately, many choices arise. How frequently should you call? Is the bird approaching or just gobbling at you? If he stops gobbling, what happened? What message are you sending? Should you move or stay put? These questions loom even larger when working pressured turkeys.

First—as always—start with soft calling, even if you're not supertight to a gobbler. If a turkey responds and reacts to soft, subtle calling, let him. He's probably pepper-hot. Sometimes soft yelping, a few clucks, and low-key clucking and purring are the ticket.

But if you must, don't be afraid to get louder and more aggressive. Some gobblers seem to ratchet up their intensity when hit with cutting and loud yelping. (This generally isn't the case with pressured turkeys,

When a tom is gobbling and moving toward you, it's usually best to call just enough to keep tabs on him and keep him coming. The "perfect" turkey gobbles and moves steadily. TES RANDLE JOLLY

but you never know.) But remember, start soft, and work your way up as needed. The turkey's response will tell you when you've hit the right mix.

Take your calling frequency cue from the turkey (veteran hunters call this "taking a bird's temperature"). If a longbeard is gobbling at every call, you can probably call a lot—maybe even every thirty seconds to a minute—without messing things up. You probably shouldn't, though. The more you make a turkey gobble, the better the odds he'll attract a real hen or another hunter—especially in hard-hunted areas. Further, calling a lot makes it much easier for a gobbler to pinpoint you, which leaves little room for error when the bird gets close.

When a tom is gobbling and moving toward you, it's usually best to call just enough to keep tabs on him and keep him coming. The "perfect" turkey gobbles and moves steadily.

Conversely, when a gobbler only answers now and then, tone down your calling. You might get him to gobble by calling a lot, but that only tells him the hen is hot to trot and will come to him. If he's only responding to every third or fourth series of calls, back off, and don't hammer him. Try calling sparingly; say about every three to five minutes.

By not calling frequently, you put the power of curiosity on your side. It's never a bad idea to get a bird fired up and then go quiet, making him hunt for the hen. This works especially well with hung-up gobblers. If a turkey gobbles in place but won't move, stop calling for fifteen minutes, and be ready. Many will eventually break and come in for a look. Pressured turkeys probably won't break right away, though. Often, they'll prolong the process, so be patient. If you decide to go silent, sit tight for at least a half-hour to an hour, trying to catch a silent strutter slipping into the area.

Incidentally, you can call in any turkey with yelps and clucks. However, it never hurts to throw in other calls. Purring works especially well to reassure hung-up gobblers that the "hen" is just over the rise, waiting for them. Further, I've also seen kee-kees—a call typically associated with fall hunting—get birds to respond when nothing else worked. Why? I don't know. Maybe it was late in the breeding season, and the kee-kees of young turkeys made those gobblers think some jennies were ready to breed. That's probably reading way too much into it. Whatever the reason, it worked.

Be prepared for contingencies, too. Some gobblers respond to anything (or sometimes, nothing!). But many times, longbeards seem to hone in on one call or sound. You've probably noticed that, if you've worked birds with a partner. A gobbler might jump all over the yelps from your box call but clam up tight when your pal clucks on a slate. Why? Maybe it's pitch or tone. Or perhaps, the bird might think he recognizes the "hen" that's calling to him. Conversely—and this is often the case—the sound might be new to him, and he's simply inviting the "new hen" to join the party.

The point is that you should have several calls ready when working a turkey. If a bird is gobbling at your mouth calling, stick with it. But if he seems to lose interest, try a box, tube, or friction call. You never know what sound will spur his interest and break him.

Also, don't be startled when a bird responds. Be ready to answer him and continue your conversation. If a gobbler cuts you off, it means he's

You should have several calls ready when working a turkey. If a bird is gobbling at your mouth calling, stick with it. But if he seems to lose interest, try a box, wingbone, or friction call. You never know what sound will spur his interest and break him.

very interested. Likewise, if a bird gobbles and you immediately yelp or cutt back at him, you're responding directly to his mating call and probably firing him up further.

Think about your next series of calls and the ones after that, too. If a longbeard climbs all over your yelping, answer him back with more. Then, be ready to hammer out some cutting as he heats up. All the while, gauge the situation—the gobbler's temperature, his distance, how fast he's approaching—and be ready to stop calling or tone things down when you need to.

It should go without saying, but concentrate on realism when working a bird. Don't break from two minutes of soft purring into a din of hellacious cutting. Ratchet up your intensity slowly. Also, don't just blurt out the same monotone yelps and clucks time after time. The yelps of real hens rise and fall in volume and intensity. Make your calling sound pleading or excited; put emotion into it. Likewise, cast your calling to one direction or another. This will make it seem like the hen is moving.

THE TOUGHEST CALL

Every once in a while, you'll pick the perfect setup, work a hot turkey, and consummate the hunt in grand fashion. But much more often, something will happen to make you question your setup. Maybe a bird just gobbles in place and doesn't approach. Perhaps he approaches but seems to hang up. Or a bird might fire up but then seem to lose interest. Is it your calling? Is it your setup? What should you do?

To move or stay put during the heat of battle—that's the toughest decision in turkey hunting. If you sit tight while a long-spurred gobbler slowly works in, you're a wise sage. But if you camp out and the bird drifts away, you're a blundering buffoon. If you make the right move at the right time on a hung-up bird, you're a master strategist. Yet if you stand up and bump that turkey, you're an impatient, overaggressive fool.

You'll find plenty of published advice on the question, but much of it might seem contradictory. Many pros advocate a hard-charging style, and they kill loads of turkeys. But just as many preach patience and caution, and they also kill lots of gobblers. In truth, you won't find many hard-and-fast answers. Much of the decision about whether to move or sit tight depends on your personality, the terrain, and the mood of the turkeys.

In general, many hunters move far too quickly. They lack patience or confidence in their setup, calling, or pre-season scouting. Remember, planning and patience kill turkeys. Calling is just the medium. This is especially true with pressured gobblers. If a turkey is interested in your calling and you're confident in your plan and setup, it's probably wise to

To move or stay put during the heat of battle—that's the toughest decision in turkey hunting. If you sit tight while a long-spurred gobbler slowly works in, you're a wise sage. But if you camp out and the bird drifts away, you're a blundering buffoon.

stay put and wait the bird out. However, that's a huge generalization, and simply sitting tight won't work every time.

The key is awareness. If you can determine why a bird isn't committing or where he's going, you're way ahead of the game. If you can't, you might have to guess.

When a gobbler suddenly goes silent, sit tight and be ready. Odds are he's walking in. Just listen for drumming, and watch for that softball head bobbing through the woods. Really, moving in this situation does no good. After all, you're not sure where that gobbler is! And if you don't know where he's at, moving is a sure way to bump him. Sit tight for a while or until you get a fix on him again.

If nothing happens after a while—wait at least fifteen minutes but preferably a half-hour—cutt aggressively or use a locator call to make the bird shock-gobble. If that doesn't work, you should probably try to find another turkey.

If a longbeard suddenly hangs up but continues gobbling, sit tight for a bit. You'll be tempted to hammer him, but it's best to switch to soft stuff or stop altogether. That will play on the bird's curiosity and might make him break and come in. Wait at least twenty minutes to a half-hour, and

In general, many hunters move far too quickly. They lack patience or confidence in their setup, calling, or pre-season scouting. Remember, planning and patience kill turkeys.

keep the faith. Something will happen eventually, whether the bird comes in, walks off, or hooks up with a hen. Just be ready to identify the situation and adapt to it.

Of course, if being patient and sitting tight doesn't work, you'll have to move. Maybe a bird's approach is blocked by some obstacle, or perhaps the turkey just doesn't want to come to your setup. Ease away from your tree, and—without calling—slip to a new spot that might let the bird approach more easily, whether it's a ridge above the gobbler or an open flat or bench nearby. Sometimes, a quick change of scenery is all it takes.

Further, even if your covert move doesn't improve your calling position much, it accomplishes something important: it gives the illusion of movement. After all, real hens usually don't sit in one spot and call for a half-hour or more. Usually, they're walking through the woods on turkey business: feeding, going to lay an egg, or traveling to their nest.

If a bird gobbles while going away, he's telling you where to ambush him. Using your knowledge of the terrain, take your best guess at where the turkey is heading—a long ridge, field edge, timbered bottom—whatever. Then, slip around the turkey, find a likely setup, and call softly and sparingly—if at all.

If a longbeard suddenly hangs up but continues gobbling, sit tight for a bit. You'll be tempted to hammer him, but it's best to switch to soft stuff or stop altogether. That will play on the bird's curiosity and might make him break and come in.

If the turkey moves away but shuts up, you'll just have to take your best shot. Set up where you think the turkey might be going, and give it a whirl. If nothing happens after an hour, move on.

In the end, your response to the move-or-stay question boils down to confidence. If you're in a good spot and are certain turkeys will visit the area throughout your hunt, you're not hurting yourself by staying put. If you can keep tabs on a moving gobbler and know the land well, you'll likely sneak into position and be ready for the old bird when he walks into range.

Use your head, and draw from your experiences afield. After you build a mental library of how turkeys respond in various situations, your success rate will climb. If you mess up and spook a turkey, just laugh it off and move on. Remember, every turkey hunter makes mistakes.

THE FINAL FEW YARDS

Every turkey hunter has been there. A bird responds to your calling, approaches to within 65 yards, struts and gobbles like mad, but then eventually folds up and walks away, leaving you wondering what went wrong.

No matter how well you call or maneuver through the woods, it's often tough to make gobblers "break the force field" and approach the final critical yards into range. Sometimes, there's nothing you can do, whether it's because of the situation or the mood of a bird. However, several tricks can help you convert more of those "almost" turkeys into dead birds.

Location is probably the Number One factor in luring turkeys close. Whenever possible, set up and call from areas turkeys frequent and with which they are comfortable. You should have found several of these during your scouting forays. If you yelp to a gobbler from an oak-studded bench where he likes to strut, you're in business. If you call to him from a distant cedar-dotted ridge, your chances of success decrease dramatically.

Hot turkeys sometimes work in quickly but then stop, strut, and gobble in one spot before drifting off. Often, small obstructions or terrain features halt their approach. These might include creeks, ditches, fences, swamps, or thick, brushy patches.

Identify areas where birds might hang up, and don't try to work turkeys to or through these areas. For example, if a longbeard gobbles at you across a deep hollow, don't just plop your butt down and attempt to work him down the ridge and through the bottoms. Use locator calls to keep tabs on the longbeard, and sneak around to the ridge he's on. He might run you over after your first yelp.

And again, a good setup will also help you avoid many "almost" turkeys. Try to find ideal setups; ones that conceal the source of your calling, and from where you can shoot a gobbler immediately after you see him.

Of course, you can't always find the perfect setup or move to an ideal location. Often, you're stuck trying to lure a bird across a field or through open woods. Or sometimes, even if you have a good setup, a bird might hang just over a small ridge—20 steps away but out of sight. Don't despair, because you can still score.

In open areas, birds instinctively know they should be able to see the source of calling. If they hear yelping but see no hen, they know something is amiss. Decoys help in such situations, but they're not a panacea.

If a turkey hangs up where he can see you, only call when he struts, pecks at the ground, or turns his head—never when he's eyeballing you. He'll still know where the calling is coming from, but at least he won't be staring at a suspicious "yelping stump."

Of course, less is usually more when turkeys hang up. If you play hard-to-get, he might get impatient and waltz in. It's also not a bad idea to just go silent. A gobbler will still probably come in, but he won't pin-

No matter how well you call or maneuver through the woods, it's often tough to make gobblers "break the force field" and approach the final critical yards into range. TES RANDLE JOLLY

point your location as easily, and his curiosity will prompt him to hunt for the hen. Shut up for at least fifteen minutes, and see if the gobbler breaks. If he doesn't, it might be time to move.

If a bird won't commit, you can try several relocation tactics. First, back away from the bird, and sneak to another nearby area. Maybe some unseen obstruction prevented the bird from coming to your initial setup. Often, a small change of scenery helps break the stalemate.

You might also walk away from the bird, calling as you go. After you retreat about 100 yards, stop calling, and circle back 40 or so yards. A gobbler won't charge in, but he might come closer to where he last heard the hen, and you'll be sitting in his approach lane.

If you're hunting with a partner, he can walk away from you calling, leaving you in the hot seat. The bird might not go all the way to him, but it might come closer, giving you a shot. If a bird still won't commit, it's decision time. Terrain or cover permitting, you might crawl as close as possible, ease up, and shoot the gobbler. There's nothing wrong with that—if you're certain you're alone. Don't try it on public land or heavily hunted private spots.

A good setup will also help you avoid many "almost" turkeys. Try to find ideal setups: ones that conceal the source of your calling, and where you can shoot a gobbler immediately after you see him.

If a turkey is in range but hung up just over a ridge or hill, simply stand up slowly and shoot the bird when he periscopes his head. Again, you called in the bird but merely needed an extra twist to put him in the freezer.

Even with this bag of tricks, you won't convince every hung-up bird to travel the last few critical yards within range. If you throw the works at a longbeard but he still won't budge, let him walk away, and try to circle around and cut him off. If that doesn't work, remember him for another day. He'll still be around.

And in the meantime, you might find another gobbler that will rush in and make you feel much better.

Notes from the Turkey Woods

The Road Not Crawled

Some turkeys have a pretty twisted sense of humor.

During the heat of battle, they'll present you with starkly contrasting choices. Now and then, each of those choices seems good—so good, in fact, that you almost have to flip a coin to decide how you'll fill your tag.

Or so it seems.

A couple of springs ago, a friend from West Virginia and I stood atop a high Minnesota ridge and strained our ears to hear gobbling. Finally, a bird sounded off from what seemed like a mile away. We eased closer and pinpointed the gobbler on the facing slope of a very steep, deep ravine. I wasn't thrilled about going up or down those slippery, multiflora rose-filled slopes, but the bird was hammering, so I couldn't resist.

We scampered down—almost straight down—to the creek bottom, waded the small stream, hustled through some brush-choked pasture, and huffed and puffed up—almost straight up—the opposite slope. As we neared the crest, the turkey gobbled close—almost too close—blowing our hats off.

Immediately, we dug into some nearby oaks and assessed the situation. It was almost too perfect. The bird was strutting and gobbling on an open hardwood flat atop the ridge. We were just below the lip of the ridge, probably about 60 steps from the gobbler. If we could just lure the bird 20 to 30 steps to the crest of the hill, he'd be in easy shotgun range when he poked his head up.

I nodded at my friend and then hit the slate call. The longbeard triple-gobbled. My buddy's eyes lit up as he leveled his shotgun across his knee.

"This turkey is going to run us over!" I thought.

But after several tense minutes, it became apparent that wouldn't happen. The gobbler honored all of my calls with booming responses, and his loud drumming indicated he was almost within range. However, he remained in the same spot, strutting, gobbling, and drumming in the early-morning sunlight.

After twenty minutes, the situation hadn't changed. I sighed and pondered whether to remain patient or have my buddy attempt a bushwhack. At first, the "crawl-up-to-the-ridgetop-and-shoot-him" option seemed ludicrous. After all, the bird was red-hot, and had answered almost every yelp, cluck, and purr I'd made. Further, we were in an ideal setup not 60 steps from the gobbler.

Still, long waits for hard-gobbling turkeys make me nervous. There's always a good chance that a longbeard's hammering will attract a hot little hen, which will pretty much ruin your morning. Further, my friend and I were on public land, so I worried that the bird's chatty nature would attract a larger, clumsier two-legged visitor. In addition, even pepper-hot gobblers often seem to lose steam—and interest—after twenty minutes or so, and I've learned the hard way that the longer the hunt takes, the greater your odds that something will go wrong.

A stealthy crawl and sure shot would have ended the hunt quickly. However, when I assessed that strategy, it made me even more nervous. The ridge was covered with duff and dead leaves, so any movement would be noisy. And the morning was dead calm, so the odds of approaching unheard were slim. Further, the ridgetop was very open. If the gobbler popped his head up at any time during a stalk, the hunt would be finished.

I could have whispered for my friend to slowly stand and shoot the turkey the instant he saw it, but I decided against that. The gobbler might have been close enough to shoot, but there was no way to be sure. And after my friend stood, that would be it.

Finally, memories of past mistakes made my decision easy. Patience and positioning are usually the critical elements when dealing with an obstinate turkey, and we already had the latter. I just needed to exercise the former.

I decided to wait that old buzzard out. I yelped and clucked again, sending him into a gobbling frenzy. Then, I stuck my striker in my pocket, looked at my watch and vowed not to call again for fifteen minutes. Common sense dictated that there was no way a piping-hot gobbler would walk away without at least peeking over the ridge to check out the hen that had driven him wild.

At first, the situation played out as expected. The bird continued to rip it and filled the woods with spitting and drumming. Now and then, we heard his wings smack the ground as he strutted.

I raked leaves with my hands, trying to mimic a feeding hen. He gobbled. Finally, I called softly. He gobbled. I called more aggressively and then shut up for several more minutes. It didn't matter. He gobbled. But he would not budge.

That went on for almost an hour, and every time the turkey went silent, I expected to see that white softball periscope above the ridge.

It never did. Eventually, the bird moved to our left, but he was farther away. When another gobble confirmed the turkey was going the wrong way, my friend and I slipped to the ridgetop and gave chase.

It didn't matter. He was gone.

I had chosen to be patient, dug my heels in, and resolved to wait. And the longbeard had dug his hind toes in, gobbled his brains out, and finally moved to greener pastures.

"Maybe you should have belly-crawled him," I said sheepishly to my friend.

He sighed and shook his head.

"Maybe so," he replied.

Not exactly a vote of confidence.

After twenty minutes, the situation hadn't changed. I sighed and pondered whether to remain patient or have my buddy attempt a bushwhack.

A week later in Wisconsin, my buddy Jay Greene and I set up on two long-beards that acted almost like that Minnesota curmudgeon. They gobbled like crazy, but strutted and drummed just out of sight. And each time, I called sparingly and remained patient, confident that they would eventually break and present a shot.

The result? Two filled tags, two early breakfasts, and satisfaction from knowing patience had been the right call, at least during those hunts.

Those birds made me feel somewhat better about the Minnesota disaster. Still, I couldn't help but wonder if a crawl might have been the better option. ⚡

CHAPTER 9

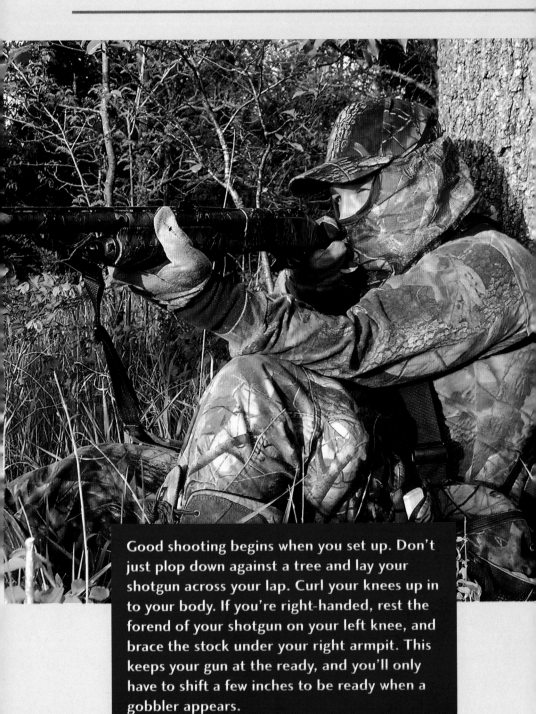

Good shooting begins when you set up. Don't just plop down against a tree and lay your shotgun across your lap. Curl your knees up in to your body. If you're right-handed, rest the forend of your shotgun on your left knee, and brace the stock under your right armpit. This keeps your gun at the ready, and you'll only have to shift a few inches to be ready when a gobbler appears.

Finishing the Deal

When I told the story afterward, the hunt sounded like a slam-dunk. And really, it had been classic—at least until the shot.

My buddy Jay Greene and I had walked into a long timbered ridge that rose to a high-top stubble field. A bird had hammered 60 yards away and had flown down almost within range. He'd honored the two or three strings of yelps I sent his way, and then gobbled and drummed just out of sight over the ridge for what seemed like eternity. I knew he'd pop up for a look at some point, but that's when things got interesting.

At about 30 steps, the bird periscoped his head and looked for the hen. Trouble was, his head—and only his head—was barely visible through a large brush pile between us. And knowing the bird would quickly determine there wasn't a hen where he'd heard the calling, I had to do something quickly.

As slowly as possible, I eased my gun to the right, trying to squeeze the barrel under a low-hanging branch and keep my face on the stock. When my fiber-optic sights intersected with the gobbler's neck, I steadied myself for a second and squeezed the trigger.

Bang. Dead turkey.

I heaved a sigh of relief and chased the dead-yet-flopping gobbler down the steep ridge. When I retrieved him, I thought about everything that could have gone wrong: having to move my gun, shoot through an obstruction, and make a split-second decision about when to fire. Had I jerked or moved too quickly, the gobbler would have spooked. If I had stayed motionless and waited for a better shot, the bird would have

When a gobbler gets relatively close—that is, he's almost in range or will be there soon—you should have your gun in firing position. If you see a turkey from afar or track it via gobbling or drumming, this isn't difficult. TES RANDLE JOLLY

walked away. And unless my aim and timing had been on, I could have shot brush or a tree, sending the longbeard flying into the next county.

Years earlier, that gobbler probably would have walked away. But after a couple of decades of chasing turkeys, I guess I'd learned a lesson or two about how and when to shoot them.

THE APPROACH

On the surface, shooting a turkey seems simple: see the bird, aim at its neck, and fire. But as any veteran turkey hunter knows, the game rarely plays out so easily. Shooting a gobbler usually requires more thought, savvy, and experience—plus a cool head.

Good shooting begins when you set up. Don't just plop down against a tree and lay your shotgun across your lap. Curl your knees up in to your body. If you're right-handed, rest the forend of your shotgun on your left knee, and brace the stock under your right armpit. This keeps your gun at the ready, and you'll only have to shift a few inches to be ready when a gobbler appears.

Many people face directly toward a turkey or where they think a gobbler will approach. This is also a mistake. If you're right-handed, point your left shoulder and the gun barrel toward the turkey. In this position, you'll be able to swing to your left or right. If you face the turkey, you cannot swing to your right if an approaching longbeard veers off course.

FINDING YOUR IDEAL PATTERN

Your shotgun's pattern determines its in-field effectiveness. To optimize the performance of your gun, pattern it extensively before the season. If you can afford it, test various brands of shotshells, plus different loads and shot sizes. Usually, a clear favorite will emerge.

Many folks pattern their guns using a 30-inch circle at 30 yards. This is a great way to start. Any gun and choke that places 100 or more pellets inside that 30-inch circle at 30 steps is a real shooter.

I use a slightly different method. I place a Birchwood-Casey Shoot-n-See target at 20 steps from the bench and fire one shot to make sure my gun's point of impact is on. If it is, I place several targets at 30 steps. Here's where you really test the pattern.

I then fire my gun at three targets and compare the results to get an average of its performance. First, I note the consistency of my pattern. Is it even? If it has holes or clumps of pellet marks, that might cause problems in the field. If so, my choke and load might not be ideally matched.

Next, I count the pellet holes. Ideally, at 30 steps, a turkey gun should place at least 35 pellets in the head and neck and at least 13 in the brain and spine. That might seem like a lot, but not every one of those 13 pellets will actually penetrate the brain and spine. I try to hedge my bets with multiple hits.

When I'm satisfied with my pattern at 30 steps, I try a shot at 40. A gun and choke that places 35 pellets in the head and neck at 30 steps will usually put 28 to 30 in a target at 40 yards. If my pattern remains even and consistent, I figure I'm in good shape. If not, I limit my shots to 35 yards or closer.

One note: turkey guns and loads kick like mules, and flinching can sabotage your pattern. Concentrate on making your first shot count.

To optimize the performance of your gun, pattern it extensively before the season. If you can afford it, test various brands of shotshells, plus different chokes, loads, and shot sizes. Usually, a clear favorite will emerge.

THERE HE IS!

When a gobbler gets relatively close—that is, he's almost in range or will be there soon—you should have your gun in firing position. If you see a turkey from afar or track it via gobbling or drumming, this isn't difficult. Simply ready your gun as the turkey approaches. When he's in range and looking for the "hen," you'll be on him.

As a gobbler approaches—whether you're tracking him by sound or watching him—move with him. That might sound like blasphemy, but think about it. It's rare that a bird walks right into your firing line. You have to move somewhat to shoot almost every longbeard, whether it's making final adjustments with your gun or following a walking turkey. Moving with the bird as it approaches eliminates the need for big adjustments when the moment of truth arrives. Some hunters call this "flowing with the turkey." You're simply moving your gun and shifting your body at the same pace at which a gobbler is moving.

If a bird gobbles slightly to the right of your gun barrel, slowly ease your body to the right. If he then gobbles back to the left, slowly shift again. This way, you can follow him all the way in. Even if you see an approaching bird, don't be afraid to flow with him. Just ease your body and barrel with the turkey. He won't catch the subtle movement. Of course, if he stops and periscopes his head, glaring at you with those evil eyes, remain still.

By flowing with the bird until he's in range, you'll usually just have to cluck or wait till the gobbler sticks his head up. Then, it's time to shoot. Of course, you can't always do that. Sometimes, birds come in silently or take you by surprise when your gun is down. Don't panic, and resist the temptation to take a snap shot.

If the bird is staring at you, stay still. As he begins to walk, look for trees, brush, or other obstacles between you and the bird that might obscure his vision. As he passes behind them, mount your gun swiftly and decisively. If there's no cover, don't worry. If the bird is strutting, wait till he turns away and obscures his vision with his fan. Quickly shoulder your gun. Or, as the bird starts to strut, peck, or walk, ease the gun to your shoulder as slowly as you can. He won't catch it.

One final note: often, turkeys don't cooperate quickly, so you might have to keep your gun ready for many agonizing minutes. Your arms will ache, your forearms will burn, and your hands will start to shake. The best advice I can offer is to keep your mind on the prize. If the turkey can see—or even hear—you, any swift, unsteady movements to alleviate your burning arms will spook him. Keep that in mind, fight through the fatigue, and concentrate on the hunt. If you must rest your arms for a

When do you shoot? That sounds like a ridiculous question, but many hunters fail that exam every spring by shooting at birds out of range or letting them get too close. TES RANDLE JOLLY

Even if you see an approaching bird, don't be afraid to flow with him. Just ease your body and barrel with the turkey. He won't catch the subtle movement. Of course, if he stops and periscopes his head, glaring at you with those evil eyes, remain still.

minute, try to lower the gun as slowly as possible to your knee. Then, after a quick breather, remount the shotgun slowly.

FINAL DETAILS

Let's assume a turkey is working in steadily, and you're flowing with him. It's all systems go, and he'll soon be in range. But when do you shoot?

That sounds like a ridiculous question, but many hunters fail that exam every spring by shooting at birds out of range or letting them get too close. Folks often debate the best range at which to shoot a turkey, and I've seen hunters kill birds at five steps and out to 65 yards. But really, you want to kill a bird at the distance where your pattern is optimal: 20 to 35 steps. If you let a bird get too close, your pattern will be the size of a golf ball when you shoot. And if a bird is too far, your sparse pattern will probably only wound him.

First, determine your range limit. When you set up, try to pick out a tree or other landmark you think is at the edge of your range. It might be an oak at 40 steps or a large rock at 50. If time allows, step off the distance to your setup, or use a laser range-finder to nail down the range. If a turkey is equal to or within that imaginary boundary, you know he's in

The best advice I can offer is to keep your mind on the prize. If the turkey can see—or even hear—you, any swift, unsteady movements to alleviate your burning arms will spook him.

range. You can't always do this when hunting in open areas, but practicing it every time you set up will help you better estimate range.

Also, know when to say when. If a hot bird is approaching, it seems natural to let him come as close as possible. However, birds closer than 20 steps are difficult targets. It's easy to whistle a baseball-sized pattern past their bobbing heads at 15 steps.

If an approaching bird is in good range—say 20 to 35 steps—cluck or cutt so he raises his head, and shoot him. Or, if the bird stops and raises his head in the open, offering a good shot, take it. Often, the Number One mistake turkey hunters make is not taking their first good shot.

If you've chosen your setup wisely, you might not see the turkey until he's in range. It's best to set up 25 to 35 steps from small terrain rises, bends in logging roads, or other obstacles that prevent a bird from seeing the source of calling until he's in range. When a gobbler tops a rise or rounds a bend in the road, he'll instinctively know he should be able to see the "hen," and he'll stop and raise his head—often in a two-step "double-pump" motion—to look for her. When he does that, shoot him. Don't hesitate. Otherwise, when he doesn't see the hen, he won't hang around long. He'll tuck his wing once or twice, which means he's about to walk away.

MAKIN' IT

Most hunters know to aim just above a gobbler's wattles. That way, the pattern will cover the top of his head to his upper chest, ensuring numerous pellet hits in the brain and spine. Further, if a bird ducks his head as you shoot, you'll still kill him.

The only exception to that rule might be when a gobbler gets too close. If you're shooting at a walking turkey within 15 steps, you might want to aim low on its neck to ensure you don't miss that bobbing head.

Also, try to avoid shooting at strutting gobblers. When turkeys strut, they compress their spinal column, providing less target area than a bird with its head held high. As mentioned, birds will often break strut and crane their necks to look for a hen when they approach. If a bird continues to strut as he approaches, cluck or cutt loudly. That usually makes a gobbler drop strut and look at the source of the calling. Shoot when he raises his head. If you must shoot at a strutter, try to do it as he turns sideways to you, and aim for the base of his neck. You'll probably put a few pellets in his breast, but at least you won't "feather-pillow" him with a straight-on body shot.

After you shoot, remain vigilant. You won't always kill the turkey. Usually, the bird will collapse dead and flop around a bit. If it does not, be

Most hunters know to aim just above a gobbler's wattles. That way, the pattern will cover the top of his head to his upper chest, ensuring numerous pellet hits in the brain and spine. Further, if a bird ducks his head as you shoot, you'll still kill him. TES RANDLE JOLLY

ready for a quick follow-up shot. Many missed turkeys are startled or confused momentarily, and they might just jump or fly a few feet before craning their neck to see what happened. If a tom does that, readjust your gun, and kill him.

If a bird flies, resist the temptation to take a flyer at him. You've missed, and wounding a flying turkey will only make things worse. Let him go, and hunt him another day. If a missed bird runs, it's probably okay to take a second shot, especially if he's fleeing directly away from you. Aim carefully, and squeeze the trigger. If he's rapidly rubber-necking at a right angle to you, act quickly, and make sure to aim at his head. You don't want to body-shoot and cripple a bird. That only makes your day worse.

continued on page 141

THOSE MISERABLE MISSES

There I was, living the dream.

Behind me was Eddie Salter, world-champion turkey caller and an undeniable legend of spring gobbler hunting. Thirty-five yards in front of me were two red-hot Alabama longbeards, strutting, spitting, and drumming their way toward my big 10-gauge.

It was like I had won the World Series—no, the Super Bowl! I would tell this tale forever. But something funny happened on the way to immortality.

As the birds criss-crossed in front of my bead, I waited for the videographer to my right to give his kill signal. And I waited some more. And then waited even longer. What the heck was going on?

Finally, the birds began to get nervous and walk away. Worse, they were headed for a row of pretty thick young trees.

"You'd better reach out there and kill one," the videographer finally said. Thanks.

I eased to my right, tried to steady the wobbling bead on the head of the trailing gobbler and jerked the trigger. Ker-pow! Brush exploded everywhere, and the longbeards ran off unharmed. I stared in disbelief—I'd missed!

Salter walked up to me, half grinning and half shaking his head. I think he knew what had happened, but I wasn't about to blame the camera man. I'd been the guy behind the trigger.

"Well, that'll happen," Salter said in his gentlemanly Southern drawl. "We'll just go find another."

Of course, you've no doubt guessed that we did not find another during that trip. And my miss lives in infamy.

The best thing to do after missing a turkey is to collect yourself, identify any mistakes you made, and move on. Replay the hunt in your head, and figure out where you went wrong.

Those Miserable Misses, continued

I've learned since that it's easy to miss a turkey. Just ask me; I've done 'em all. Shoot brush or another obstruction? Yep. Take your head off the stock? Check. Rush the shot or jerk the trigger? You bet. Shoot too far? Oh yeah. Let a bird get too close? Uh huh. Just plain psyche yourself out? Several times.

Like I said, I'm a turkey missing expert. But do you know what? If you haven't missed a few turkeys, you're a liar, or you haven't hunted them much. It happens to everyone, including all the big-name callers and pro-staffers we turkey hunters idolize. Many—and I'm a member of this sorry club—have missed two turkeys in a day.

Really, missing a turkey is much like a quarterback throwing over the head of an open receiver. Had he simply used his head, taken his time, and delivered the ball as he had many times before, the pass would have been completed. Likewise, turkey hunters often get nervous, rattled, or otherwise careless when they miss.

Sometimes, misses can't be avoided. If you shoot a sapling or hit an unseen gooseberry bush, what can you do? Try to identify these and other trouble spots, of course, but don't dwell on it if you shoot one instead of your gobbler.

The best thing to do after missing a turkey is to collect yourself, identify any mistakes you made, and move on. Replay the hunt in your head, and figure out where you went wrong. Did you set up incorrectly? Were you excited, and did you rush the shot? Had you waited too long for the "perfect" shot and then taken a subpar shot?

If you think your gun or sights might be off, go to the range, and double-check everything. Then, assuming your shooting iron is functioning correctly, just forget about the miss. Realize that it's part of turkey hunting and that you'll do better next time. And when that gobbler works within range the next day, do what you've trained yourself to do: shoot him.

Remember that dreaded two-misses-in-one-day club? I joined the fraternity in 1998 during a Minnesota hunt. I'd taken a long-distance poke at a strutter one morning and then inexplicably missed a walking tom later that day. The next day, I borrowed a friend's gun and, to make a long story short, ended up on my belly just nine steps from a longbeard in a cattle pasture.

I almost bored a hole in the neck of that turkey, making sure my friend's Holo sight was dead on the bird's wattles. And I never squeezed a trigger so perfectly. When the gun fired, I gritted my teeth, whispered a silent prayer, jumped up and saw the dead bird flopping in the morning sun.

No doubt, you'll have similar experiences. Just remember that many kills will follow those few misses.

If your shot seems like a clean, classic kill, don't get caught up in the excitement of the moment. Keep your gun ready, stand up, and calmly approach your turkey. Many folks—myself included—jump up like they've been shot from a cannon and spring toward a dead bird. In the old days, before modern chokes and shotshells turned shotguns into turkey-smoking machines, hunters often had to race to their birds to make sure they got a boot on its neck. Nowadays, unless you make a poor shot or are using the wrong equipment, this simply isn't necessary.

Watch the bird. If it's dead or flopping, keep your gun ready and walk to him. If the bird puts its head up, beat a path to him, and get your foot on his neck. Or, if he seems ready to escape, shoot him again. It's better to have a perforated gobbler in your truck than a mortally wounded longbeard slinking about the woods.

The moment of truth makes many folks nervous, but with every turkey you kill, you learn how to calm yourself. Take deep breaths, follow the bird and shoot at the appropriate time. Your heart won't beat out of your chest, even though that might seem likely.

Above all, enjoy it. Working a close bird is the essence of the hunt. Gently squeeze the trigger and retrieve your gobbler, knowing you've finished the grand game in splendid fashion.

Watch the bird. If it's dead or flopping, keep your gun ready, and walk to him. If the bird puts its head up, beat a path to him, and get your foot on his neck. Or if he seems ready to escape, shoot him again.

Notes from the Turkey Woods

Goof-Up Redux

Pat Reeve, Scott Bestul, and I plopped our butts down by three big field-edge oaks and started calling. We'd worked a bird in the area early that morning, and after a brief midmorning rain shower, we were set to try him again.

Sure enough, the tom gobbled at our calls. He was still there. But suddenly, Bestul hissed, "He's coming! He's coming!"

I couldn't believe it. A gobbler and two hens waltzed up from the hollow, craned their necks to see the source of the calling, and proceeded to go about their turkey business just down the hill from us. As they angled toward us but to the right, Reeve captured all the great footage on film.

After a couple of minutes, I was getting nervous. The birds had heard our calling and seen our decoys, but they sure weren't committing. In fact, they were drifting farther right, and if they continued, they'd be out of our lives forever. I guessed the gobbler at about 45 steps, figured I'd better take my best shot and squeezed the trigger.

Crack! The sound of thumping wings filled the air, and the turkeys were gone in an instant. All that remained was one wingfeather. I'd missed!

It turned out my "45 yards" was really 57. Further, after reviewing the footage, I'd shot low, spraying the grass near the gobbler but leaving him apparently unharmed.

"No harm done," Reeve said. "We'll just go find another gobbler."

Yeah, right. Things like that never happened to me.

So, you can imagine my surprise at about 11:30 A.M. when we cranked up another gobbler on the opposite end of the property. In fact, we ended up slipping to within 60-some yards of the big boy as he strutted in a plowed field and battled three jakes. Back then, Minnesota's season closed at noon, so we didn't have much time.

Thankfully, the turkey made our decision easy by leaving the jakes and walking right down a fence line toward us. He's pass through a gap 40 steps away, and I could shoot him right there.

"Are you ready?" Reeve whispered.

"Yep," I said, not really believing myself.

Soon, the bird's bobbing head and neck appeared in the gap, and I fired. The gobbler jumped and ran.

I fired again. The gobbler flew.

I fired again. The gobbler kept flying, perhaps a bit quicker.

As I continued calling at the gobbler, Scott Bestul hissed, "He's coming!"
TES RANDLE JOLLY

Thinking I might have hit the bird, I gave chase to a wooded draw, leaving my apparently useless gun in the plowed field. Of course, I never saw any sign of the turkey. I'd missed again—and it had been captured on tape again.

Dejected, I walked back into the field to retrieve my boat anchor . . . er, gun. Scott tried to make me feel better by saying things like, "It happens to everyone," and "You'll get the next one." He's a heck of a nice guy, but he's a darned poor liar.

Pat just shook his head, probably wondering what kind of a putz he'd hooked up with. We hunted together quite a bit in those days, so I'm sure he eventually figured out he'd associated with a major putz.

But do you know what? Scott was right. I killed a turkey the next day. And although I've missed some turkeys since then, I haven't missed many. Some days just ain't your day, and when it happens, you can only resolve to improve.

Oh, what about that great footage Pat shot? The scenes of me missing two gobblers in one morning? Did it ever see the light of day?

Certainly. Do you think I have such a huge ego that I'd try to hide that? The footage was used on a pilot for what was to be Wisconsin Outdoor Journal television, hosted—regrettably—by yours truly.

Never saw the pilot? That's a shame. I know where a few copies might be . . . tucked away in a locked safe in my basement. !<

When longbeards get henny, you must adjust, stay focused, and stay the course. Tactics for dealing with henned-up turkeys vary somewhat depending on the phase of the breeding cycle.

Troubleshooting the Tough Ones

The title of this chapter is something of a misnomer. After all, turkeys are inherently tough to hunt. If you're chasing pressured gobblers, your job becomes increasingly difficult.

And just when things seem darkest, turkeys pile it on by going silent, acting weird, getting henned-up, or just otherwise going into a funk. The already tough task of killing a pressured turkey seemingly escalates from very difficult to mission impossible.

There's good news and bad news here. The bad news is that during the spring season, you'll almost always encounter those super-tough situations. The good news is that you can still kill those turkeys.

Let's examine several tough scenarios and how to deal with them.

HENNED-UP GOBBLERS

Now and then, I give turkey hunting seminars near my home in east-central Wisconsin. One year, a friend introduced me to the audience at his gun club by saying, "Brian's going to talk about henned-up gobblers. Well, I figure all we have to do is learn how to prevent gobblers from getting henned-up, and we won't need to learn anything else."

That statement, albeit absurd and impossible, was true. If hunters could somehow stop gobblers from finding hens every spring, turkey hunting would be much less challenging. But alas, that ain't gonna happen. In fact, in the current glory days of spring gobbler hunting, with record populations throughout the turkey's range, it seems gobblers have a much easier time finding and staying with hens. Maybe my friend Mark

If you stumble on a strutter with hens, simply stick with them—tracking them visually or by sound—and try to slip ahead of them or into an otherwise good setup position. TES RANDLE JOLLY

Drury summed it up best: "There are so many hens nowadays, it seems gobblers get henned-up in February and stay that way until July."

It sure seems that way sometimes. But like it or not—and you shouldn't—you must live with it. When longbeards get henny, you must adjust, stay focused, and stay the course.

Tactics for dealing with henned-up turkeys vary somewhat depending on the phase of the breeding cycle. During the gobbling peak, which typically occurs in mid- to late April in the North but much earlier—often before the season opens—in the South, gobblers are fired up and hens aren't yet serious about breeding. Toms are often very susceptible to calling because they haven't been hunted and most hens want nothing to do with them. However, that often doesn't deter many big boys from strutting over disinterested ladies. During this period, you can use three tactics to score.

The first tactic is simple and can work throughout spring. If you stumble on a strutter with hens, simply stick with them—tracking them visually or by sound—and try to slip ahead of them or into an otherwise good setup position.

If the terrain allows, this can be easier than it sounds. For example, if a flock is slowly moving northward along a ridge, you can obviously drop off the ridge, circle around to the north, find a likely setup 100 or so yards ahead of the flock, and then set up. Likewise, if birds are moving along a finger ridge that intersects a larger perpendicular ridge, you can zip ahead of them, find a good-looking spot on the main ridge, and take your chances. Often in such scenarios, you won't even have to call.

Of course, this is more difficult in flat or open terrain. If you slip up on a breeding flock in a flat, open woods, you might have to belly-crawl at a snail's pace for 100 or more yards before you can make any kind of move. You might have to stick with the flock—sitting, crawling, or staying just within listening distance—until you can determine a course of action. If nothing else, you can always set up as close as possible to the birds and try some soft calling. It won't work often, but you never know.

If you encounter a breeding flock in a field, don't panic. Depending on the size of the field, you might be able to maneuver through the brush or timber around the opening and find a likely exit area. Remember, as

If you encounter a breeding flock in a field, don't panic. Depending on the size of the field, you might be able to maneuver through the brush or timber around the opening and find a likely exit area. TES RANDLE JOLLY

Harold Knight taught me years ago, turkeys won't usually travel from one end of a field to the other; they usually exit before that, like a football player stepping out of bounds at the 20-yard-line rather than trying to ram into the end zone. If you find a likely entry/exit area in the direction the birds are headed, slip around them, set up, and take your chances. It beats watching them in the field and feeling your blood pressure rise.

The second tactic, calling to the hens, is probably overrated and glamorized too much, but it sometimes works early in the season. During early spring, before hens are serious about breeding, they're still somewhat grouped up and sorting out their pecking order. As such, you can often provoke a curious or even aggressive response from a hen by calling to her.

Sometimes, some soft yelping, clucking, and purring will attract a hen or group of hens out of curiosity. You never know if big daddy will be in tow. Other times, aggressive cutting and yelping will tick off the boss hen, and she might start yapping back at you, assume an aggressive posture, and walk through the woods looking to run off the interloper. This doesn't work often, but it's magic when it does. I came whisker-close to killing a big Wisconsin strutter years ago after angering and pulling in his girlfriend.

When should you try this tactic? Well, whenever you have to, I guess. If you can't move on turkeys or break a gobbler away from his girlfriends, you might as well give it a whirl. Even if it only works once, it will be worthwhile. However, here's a word of warning: this tactic seems to work best with unpressured birds. Further, when hens are ready to breed, calling to them is poison. When deciding whether to attempt this, gauge how hens respond to your calling, and be ready to switch tactics if they ignore or seem turned off by your yelping.

The third tactic just involves trying to call a gobbler away from hens. This is often an exercise in futility and frustration. Still, I've seen it work often enough that you cannot discount it during times of desperation.

Years ago in Alabama, I followed Bo Pitman, head guide at the famed White Oak Plantation near Tuskegee, as he slithered and crawled through the muck and brambles while trailing a big breeding flock. After two hours, one submerged boot, and too many cuts to count, we were within 60 steps of the birds as they fed in a pasture. Pitman yelped softly, and lo and behold, a longbeard broke ranks, ducked under a fence, and marched to within 30 steps. After waiting till the bird cleared two feeding deer and some distant cattle, I squeezed the trigger and capped off the improbable hunt.

Late in spring, things begin to open up. Hens will start sitting on their nests, and gobblers are often alone, especially later in the morning. Still, many ol' boys find hens that are still ready to breed, birds that lost their clutch of eggs and will attempt another, or perhaps even young-of-the-year jennies.

Remember, hens aren't serious about breeding during early spring, and sometimes—albeit infrequently—gobblers take a hint and will seek out that hot-yelping hussie rather than stick with Miss Cold Shoulder.

Also—and this might be more important than the first point—calling to and getting gobbles in response from an old henned-up bird often attracts subordinate, or "fringe," gobblers early in the season. These birds, usually two-year-olds that have been whipped by more dominant toms, sometimes slip in silently in hopes of breeding a hen before the boss runs them off. So always keep your eyes and ears open for drumming, a muffled gobble, or feet shuffling in the leaves while calling to a henned-up bird.

You'll have to shift your tactics somewhat as spring progresses and peak breeding ensues. This is when hens get serious about perpetuating the species, and—surprise!—it coincides with the dreaded gobbling lull. Longbeards learn pretty quickly that they don't need to gobble after the hens really desire their company.

As with the early season, the best tactic for henned-up birds during peak breeding is to maneuver on the birds. Unlike early spring, however, you probably don't want to call to the hens. Remember, the ladies are intent on breeding. If they're with a gobbler and hear another hen, they'll often turn and march straight away with the gobbler close behind, almost as if they don't want to share "their man" with some floozy. You only have to see this once to deduce that calling to the hens is bad news during this time.

There is a small window of opportunity during peak breeding. Hens will usually go to their nests about midmorning most days and lay an egg. Sometimes when this happens, their sweetheart gobbler is left behind. If you can strike him during this time—and it's often brief; sometimes a half-hour or less—he might work in. That's why it pays to hunt hard during mid- and late morning when breeding is going full force.

Late in spring, things begin to open up. Hens will start sitting on their nests, and gobblers are often alone, especially later in the morning. Still, many ol' boys find hens that are still ready to breed, birds that lost their clutch of eggs and will attempt another, or perhaps even young-of-the-year jennies. Use the same henned-up tactics as you would during peak breeding, but watch and listen intently for changes. You never know when hens will leave a gobbler, or when a lonely cruising longbeard might hear your calling and sprint in.

If your best efforts fail—and they often do with henny gobblers—just try to learn something from the experience. Which way did the birds travel after flying down? Did they stick together or break up? Where did they hang out at midday? Did they respond to a particular locator call? The list is endless, and finding even a few answers brings you one step closer to cracking the code for killing that difficult turkey.

CODE OF SILENCE

You thought henned-up birds were infuriating? Shoot, at least they'll let out a courtesy gobble to your calling sometimes. Silent birds are the worst. Hunting a turkey that won't gobble flies in the face of the sport.

Sure, gobblers are often silent because they're with hens. I can deal with that, especially knowing that some of the tactics I just mentioned might get me within shotgun range of a longbeard. But sometimes, birds clam up for no apparent reason.

Years ago, my buddy Pat Reeve took me on my first Osceola hunt in Florida. We hunted a gorgeous private ranch that was loaded with turkeys, but after two long, frustrating days, I'd only heard a handful of gobbles and had yet to see a Florida tom while hunting.

"They're all henned-up," I said. "That's gotta be the reason."

But when we'd drive to and from lunch or mill about the ranch at midday, we saw loads of solo longbeards or pairs of lonely gobblers in

Turkeys go quiet for several reasons. As mentioned, they might be henned-up. Or bad weather shuts them down. But intense hunting pressure can also keep them quiet. And sometimes, longbeards will gobble themselves hoarse one day and then gobble maybe half as well the next day.

In relatively open areas, you can sneak and peek for turkeys. Using foliage and the terrain for cover, slip from spot to spot, glassing fields, peering into pastures, or watching other open spots where turkeys strut, feed, or travel.

fields and open timber. If the birds weren't henned-up, why weren't they talking?

Well, Pat and I never really figured it out. The last day of our hunt, we simply chose a good-looking spot, sat down, called once just to say we'd called, and then waited. Amazingly, a group of longbeards followed one hen into the clearing, and I shot a dandy strutter at 30 steps.

Turkeys go quiet for several reasons. As mentioned, they might be henned-up. Or, bad weather shuts them down. But intense hunting pressure can also keep them quiet. And sometimes, longbeards will gobble themselves hoarse one day and then gobble maybe half as well the next day. I've seen this happen across the country. Though no one knows for sure why this occurs, noted turkey hunting writer Michael Hanback might have summed it up best. He likened the phenomenon to a college football team that comes out fired up and blows the doors off an opponent one week but seems flat and lackluster the next. Perhaps the players expended so much energy the first week that they have little to give the next. Perhaps. It's the best explanation I've heard, at least, and I'm sticking to it.

Whatever the cause, silent turkeys are just plain tough. If birds don't gobble, you often don't know where they are. Further, they won't respond to calling, so your odds of boogering turkeys while blundering through the woods increase exponentially.

Tough times call for desperate measures. If turkeys won't gobble, you have to play the hand you're dealt. Walking and calling is often fruitless, so it's best to go into default mode. Find those hot-looking areas—scratched-up ridges, logging roads with fresh shoots, open timbered benches that catch the morning sun—set up, call sparingly, and be prepared to wait 'em out. If you're patient and stubborn enough, a bird might sneak in or squeak out a muffled gobble, giving you something to go on.

In relatively open areas, you can sneak and peek for turkeys. Using foliage and the terrain for cover, slip from spot to spot, glassing fields, peering into pastures, or watching other open spots where turkeys strut, feed, or travel. Good optics are a necessity because you must see those sharp-eyed devils before they see you and spook.

If you locate a gobbler or breeding flock, observe them for a while. If they're stationary, try to determine the best way to slip close and set up. If they're moving, look for a likely ambush spot, and figure out how to sneak there.

Locator calls can also shine when turkeys are otherwise silent. Sometimes, a crow or hawk call might pull a shock gobble from a bird that wouldn't even raise his head at a hen call. Remember, don't overdo it with locator calls; a little goes a long way.

It might not seem like it, but silent turkeys are still turkeys, and in spring, silent gobblers still want to get with hens. If all else fails, hunt hard through these tough periods, and be ready to respond when that obstinate bird feels like gobbling again.

THE TOUGH ROUTINE

It's a tired adage, but it's true: if a turkey does something two consecutive days, he's telling you how to kill him. Yes, but there's a flip side. If a turkey does something several consecutive days that makes it impossible to kill him, you're in trouble.

Turkeys often aren't creatures of habit. They frequently don't do the same thing two consecutive days. In fact, some folks believe turkeys don't even know what they want to do when they fly down. Often, that seems true. But now and then, birds fall into patterns. If that pattern involves a longbeard flying down on a small ridge and walking a logging road toward a cornfield, that's good news for you. If that pattern entails a longbeard pitching directly into a huge field or impassable briar patch and then shutting up for the day, it's not so good.

Still, turkeys with seemingly unbreakable patterns can be killed. After all, if they're acting consistently from day to day, it at least gives you a starting point. Yes, perhaps that evil turkey pitches into a 600-acre stubble field at fly-down. He won't stay there all day. Observe him through time, and you'll eventually notice how long he stays in the field and where he leaves.

That applies to any tough scenario. Use your knowledge of his routine, however tough, and build on it. At some point during a day or season, that gobbler will be in a spot you can hunt. And if you stick with him and find him there when he's lonely, you can turn a tough season into a great hunt.

Sometimes, tough routines are often as much the product of a hunter as a bird. Is a turkey doing the same thing day after day, making it impossible for you to kill him? Perhaps. But maybe you're hunting that turkey

It might not seem like it, but silent turkeys are still turkeys, and in spring, silent gobblers still want to get with hens. If all else fails, hunt hard through these tough periods, and be ready to respond when that obstinate bird feels like gobbling again.

the same way every day. He's probably patterned you as well as you've patterned him.

If you're getting nowhere with a turkey, change up your routine. Approach him from another direction, and use different calls. Try every trick in your turkey vest to get a different response or reaction from that bird. Sometimes, that's all it takes.

Another option for birds with tough routines is to go into predator mode. Slip into the woods long before daylight, and sneak as close as possible to the bird's roost. Keep your calls in your pocket—or even the truck—and wait for the big boy to pitch down. If his routine holds true and you're in decent position, he might hit the ground in range. If so, make sure your shotgun is ready, and send a swarm of shot toward his noggin the second he lands.

Dirty pool? Nope—good hunting. You didn't limb-lift him or even bushwhack him. Like any good predator, you simply put yourself in the best possible ambush location and took advantage of opportunity.

THE OLD ONES

Old turkeys—those razor-hooked three-, four- and even five-year-olds—often act differently than their younger brethren. They won't gobble their wattles off and sprint to calling, and are often content to gobble a bit on the roost, fly down with hens, do their thing, and avoid getting killed. (Hey, that's why they're old turkeys, right?)

A hard-hunted old turkey is one tough cookie. He probably has all the previously discussed attributes—he's silent, henned-up, and has a seemingly unbreakable routine—that define a tough bird. Further, he's seen several hunting seasons come and go, and he knows the score as much as any bird with a peanut-sized brain can know the score. To make matters worse, these bad turkeys often have other birds in the area so bullied that it seems to stifle gobbling from those subordinate birds.

If you're locked in battle with a mean old buzzard, use all the tactics I've discussed in this chapter. But above all, be patient, persistent, observant, and adaptable. Very few turkeys die of old age; something kills them. Every bird has chinks in its armor, including bad old gobblers. At some point, that turkey will be vulnerable. Maybe he'll set up shop on a tiny finger ridge you identified before the season. Perhaps he'll hook up with a hen that loves to feed on that acorn-filled bottom you found while scouting. Or maybe he'll let loose one gobble on the ground to tell you where he's going.

If you're locked in battle with a mean old buzzard, use all the tactics I've discussed in this chapter. But above all, be patient, persistent, observant, and adaptable.

Old turkeys—those razor-hooked three-, four- and even five-year-olds—often act differently than their younger brethren. They won't gobble their wattles off and sprint to calling, and are often content to gobble a bit on the roost, fly down with hens, do their thing, and avoid getting killed. (Hey, that's why they're old turkeys, right?)

The possibilities are endless, but the point is clear: stick with him, learn all you can, and be ready to try almost anything. That being said, don't get obsessed with an old turkey to the point that you waste all season trying to kill him. If a bird that's whipped you all week gobbles once but a pepper-hot newcomer howls from a nearby ridge, your choice is clear: give Mr. Newbie a go. And last, don't assume that an ultra-tough turkey is an old warrior. Sometimes, subordinate two-year-olds or even jakes might act just as elusive.

Several years ago, three-time world-champion caller Don Shipp teamed with fellow world champs Drury and Steve Stoltz to chase a turkey that had frustrated him for days. The bird stuck to a wooded creek bottom, gobbling now and then but never approaching. One day, Drury and Stoltz called to the bird from a high point while Shipp slipped close to the turkey. Soon after he spotted the bird, Shipp uttered one soft cluck, and the bird eased a few steps closer. Bam! Shipp killed the turkey instantly and was elated.

As Stoltz and Drury ran down to congratulate him and see the bad bird, Shipp said, "If he's a two-year-old, you can kiss my (posterior)." But sure enough, the bird wore nubby $3/4$-inch spurs; a classic two-year-old that acted twice his age.

Notes from the Turkey Woods

Tackling the Semi-Tough

My buddy called it The Quarry. After three days, I called it Heart-
break Ridge. That really wasn't a clever title, but it sure reflected the truth.

"It" was a long, open timbered ridge that stretched south from a swampy
area. It was bordered by a large stubble field to the east and a gravel quarry to
the west. It always held turkeys, and they almost always gobbled. But could I kill
one there? Shoot, I think my chances of getting hit by lightning—which almost
happened there once, incidentally—were better.

The ridge was part of a property owned by my friend's grandparents, and
they had graciously given me permission to hunt turkeys there one spring.
Another friend and I scouted the ridge the night before the season and saw
three longbeards poking around in the gravel pit.

"Man, I know where we're going to be tomorrow morning!" I said to my
friend.

And sure enough, we were there before dawn the next day . . . along with a
trespasser who drove his truck right through the gravel pit, pretty much stifling
any gobbling that morning.

No matter. We returned the second morning, and four birds started hammering pretty hard. One continued gobbling after he hit the ground, but he drifted
east with a hen, and we never tracked him down. Figuring the turkeys were still in
the area, I told my friend we should sneak into the ridge, set up, and call softly
for an hour or two, which we did. Nothing.

The third day, we listened from the eastern edge of the ridge, and again,
four birds struck up the band. But like before, they clammed up after fly-down
and seemed to melt into the rolling slopes of the open ridge. Disgusted, we
hiked away from the ridge, and I ended up killing a gobbler in a nearby creek
bottom.

My buddy still had a tag, though, so we returned for Day 4. Same story. The
birds were roosted farther south than before, but they gobbled well on the limb,
flew down, shut up, and disappeared. I tried everything—blind-calling, walking
and calling, spotting and stalking—but we never had a clue where those gobblers went.

A week later, the friend whose grandparents owned the farm had a tag, and I
offered to accompany him. We listened from the eastern side of the ridge, and—
you guessed it—four gobblers started ripping it up before daylight. I tried to
approach them from a different angle, but we soon realized we couldn't get very
close, so we decided to try them from the pasture near the gravel pit.

After trying to figure out those tough turkeys for four miserable days, we'd stumbled into a five-minute hunt. Tough turkeys? I knew it. My friend knew it. But you could never convince my other buddy of that.

As we slipped through the swamp, hens yelped and clucked from treetops not 50 yards away. Suddenly, a booming gobble erupted from the rocky pasture in front of us. There was already a gobbler in the field!

My friend and I hit the dirt and slowly peeked into the foggy field. Sure enough, the big strutter was just 50-some steps ahead of us, barely visible in the morning haze. I lowered my head, told my friend to get ready and yelped on a diaphragm call.

"Gggggggaaaaaaarrrrrrrrrrobbbbbble!"

The bird was red-hot, but would he come? Sure enough, I heard his drumming inch closer, and I soon saw my friend's chest start to heave. I clucked and purred softly, and then put my call in my pocket. Seconds later, a shot broke the morning silence.

I jumped up, war-whooped, and rushed out to see the gobbler. I didn't have to go far; my buddy had shot him at about five steps! Better, it was only five minutes after legal shooting hours.

After trying to figure out those tough turkeys for four miserable days, we'd stumbled into a five-minute hunt. Tough turkeys? I knew it. My friend knew it. But you could never convince my other buddy of that. ✂

CHAPTER 11

Turkey hunting is not inherently dangerous. It's far safer, in terms of injuries per 100,000 participants, than soccer, tennis, and even playing pool!

Staying Safe in the Pressured Turkey Woods

This might be the most boring chapter of this book. It might also be the most important. Turkey hunters hear a lot about safety. It's hammered into our consciousness when we take hunter's safety courses, attend turkey hunting seminars, or even just chat with fellow gobbler nuts. Everyone thinks about safety, and most hunters practice it afield.

Further, despite what some folks say, turkey hunting is not inherently dangerous. It's far safer, in terms of injuries per 100,000 participants, than soccer, tennis, and even playing pool! But even though 99.5 percent of turkey hunters are safety-minded, it only takes one careless bad apple to turn the turkey woods into a place of pain, horror, and even death. And if you're hunting pressured turkeys, that usually means you're sharing the woods with other folks. You must concentrate on staying safe and watching out for the other guy.

WHAT THE NUMBERS SAY

The Fall and Winter 2000 issues of *Turkey & Turkey Hunting* magazine, a publication for which I was the editor at that time, published a groundbreaking two-part reader safety survey by then-associate editor Jennifer West. Almost 800 readers responded, and most were from heavily hunted states such as Pennsylvania, New York, Wisconsin, and Missouri.

The results were eye-opening: Almost 9 percent of respondents had been shot at, and about 2 percent had been hit or injured by shots! About 58 percent of respondents said they had been approached by other hunters while calling or using decoys, and some said that had occurred several times.

The stories from the unfortunate 2 percent were staggering. One man had been struck by eighteen pellets, three of which came within a fraction of an inch of his chest and brain.

A Pennsylvania reader had been struck in the chest and head by fifteen to eighteen pellets. He lost his right eye. Another reader was shot in the head, back, and side. He suffered permanent kidney and liver damage, and still carries 30 to 35 pellets in his body.

And another hunter was struck with 90 to 120 No. 4 pellets, which penetrated his skull and the left side of his body. He was left with epilepsy, a permanent limp, and problems with his right hand.

The stories continued: permanent damage, collapsed lungs, and pellets lodged in skull plates. And remember, these were folks who survived. Every year, a few turkey hunters are shot and killed.

Only 15 percent of respondents involved in hunting accidents knew each other, and 78 percent didn't realize there was another hunter in the area.

When asked what they believed caused or contributed most to the accident, 27.3 percent of respondents blamed stalking or sneaking. About

Although 99.5 percent of turkey hunters are safety-minded, it only takes one careless bad apple to turn the turkey woods into a place of pain, horror, and even death. And if you're hunting pressured turkeys, that usually means you're sharing the woods with other folks. You must concentrate on staying safe and watching out for the other guy.

Some folks mistakenly paint turkey hunting as a dangerous activity because participants camouflage and conceal themselves and then mimic the sounds of turkeys. That is true. However, that can never justify a shooting incident.

22.7 percent blamed hen-calling, 15.3 percent said trespassing, and 12.7 percent listed "other" causes. Failing to identify the target, gobbler-calling, failure to identify the area beyond the target, decoys, and an improper setup were blamed by 9.4 percent, 4.2 percent, 4.2 percent, 2.6 percent, and 1.6 percent of respondents, respectively. None blamed a misfire or accidental discharge.

These folks weren't neophytes, either. On average, respondents had hunted turkeys for 15 years, and spent 74 hours hunting turkeys in spring and 30 hours in fall. Almost 60 percent had taken a hunter education course. Sixty-six percent said they were very concerned about turkey hunting safety, and 28.6 percent were somewhat concerned.

Obviously, the *T&TH* survey respondents kept safety on their minds while hunting. Still, trouble had found almost one in ten of them.

Anyone who mistakenly shoots a turkey hunter is reckless, plain and simple.
There is no excuse, rationale, or justification for having done so. The only
explanation is that shooting-incident perpetrators were greedy and negligent.

STATING THE OBVIOUS

Some folks mistakenly paint turkey hunting as a dangerous activity because participants camouflage and conceal themselves, and then mimic the sounds of turkeys. That is true. However, that can never justify a shooting incident. After all, spring turkey hunters use hen calls 99 percent of the time, and, with few exceptions, hens aren't legal targets in spring. Some folks use gobbler calls now and then, but we'll touch on that later.

Further, even if a hunter is camouflaged, concealed, and yelping like a hen, no one could fathom shooting at him. After all, they have not seen—and certainly haven't positively identified—a legal gobbler!

Anyone who mistakenly shoots a turkey hunter is reckless, plain and simple. There is no excuse, rationale, or justification for having done so. The only explanation is that shooting-incident perpetrators were greedy and negligent.

So obviously, the first step to being a safe turkey hunter is to review and remind yourself of basic hunter-education principles. You've probably seen these a thousand times and practice them afield, yet they bear mention again:

1. Positively identify your target as a gobbler (or jake, if you choose). Make sure the shot path to the bird and beyond is safe.
2. Always point the muzzle of your gun in a safe direction, preferably in the air. Also, periodically check your muzzle to make sure it isn't plugged or blocked.
3. Think defensively, and assume other hunters are in the area. Never let your guard down.
4. Assume every noise or movement is another hunter.
5. Protect your back by setting up against a tree or other barrier that is wider than your shoulders and protects your head.
6. Shout loudly and clearly to alert approaching hunters. Don't wave.
7. Don't wear red, white, blue, or black clothing. Those colors are prominent on gobblers.
8. Be careful when using decoys. Set up so you're not directly in line with your decoys. That way, if an intruding hunter fires at your decoys, his shot will probably not strike you.

Basic stuff? You bet, but it's absolutely necessary. To paraphrase a famous old hunting safety poem, all the gobblers ever bred won't make up for one man dead.

Obviously, the first step to being a safe turkey hunter is to review and remind yourself of basic hunter-education principles. BRIAN DUNN

ON BUSHWHACKING

There's an old saying down South: the camo pants of any great turkey caller and hunter will always have holes in the knees. That is, even hunters who are supremely skilled at outwitting and calling in gobblers must often slip, sneak, crawl, or even swim to get a better setup or ambush a bird.

I won't delve into the so-called ethics of belly-crawling within range of a gobbler and then shooting it. I've done so many times, so I obviously have no problem with it. This chapter is about other matters, so I'll simply discuss the safety ramifications of "low-level relocation."

Whether walking or crawling, be extremely careful when slipping closer to a bird—especially a gobbling turkey. As you move toward the sound, another hunter might be doing the same. And if he catches your movement, you never know what might happen.

As you move closer to a turkey, constantly watch for other hunters or suspicious situations. Stop frequently, and assess your path and the area around you. If you see movement or hear calling, stop, try to identify the source, and don't progress until you're sure it's safe. Yes, you won't get to the turkey quite as fast, but you'll cover your safety bases.

If you're considering belly-crawling within range of a gobbler, you might reconsider. If you were on a private thousand-acre farm in Iowa, you'd probably be okay. But if you're on heavily trodden public land in Pennsylvania, you know you're not alone, so belly-crawling becomes very dangerous.

As much as we love turkey hunting, we can't let the excitement of a spring moment lure us into potentially unsafe situations. Always think about safety no matter what you're doing.

If you're considering belly-crawling within range of a gobbler, you might reconsider. If you were on a private thousand-acre farm in Iowa, you'd probably be okay. But if you're on heavily trodden public land in Pennsylvania, you know you're not alone, so belly-crawling becomes very dangerous.

I cannot tell you not to do this. After all, you might go out next spring, slip up on a public-land gobbler, and kill him without incident. I can only warn you that attempting a bushwhacking in heavily pressured areas is risky business. Exhaust all other options, and then consider hunting that turkey another day.

As much as we love turkey hunting, we can't let the excitement of a spring moment lure us into potentially unsafe situations. Always think about safety no matter what you're doing. Never stop looking for other hunters, and avoid any situation that seems potentially unsafe. You might kill a few less turkeys, but you'll be much safer.

FIELD MANEUVERS:
ANOTHER STUDY IN SAFETY DECISIONS AFIELD

There he is, strutting and drumming 55 steps away, his white head glowing like a beacon in the early-morning light.

Lying on my belly in the wet grass, I could crawl to the lip of the field edge and send a hail of lead toward the gobbler. Yet I hesitate, considering the consequences. This is a new one. I have a turkey dead to rights, and I'm not shooting.

Morning Surprise
I'd arrived in southeastern Minnesota the previous evening to hunt with good friend Scott Bestul. We quickly set out to roost gobblers, and it didn't take long. Owl-hoots from a gravel road near a large public area prompted a swift response. Bestul and a friend would hunt that turkey in the morning.

With one bird located, we cut down a nearby gravel road to a public area bordered by a farm Bestul had permission to hunt. A turkey responded to our hoots, and we plotted how I could pursue the bird the next day. The gobbler was roosted atop a ridge across from a stubble field. I could slip in by the field edge before daylight, and hopefully, the turkey would pitch down on the ridgetop and hit the field or stay along the ridge line.

The plan was solid, and it would have worked. However, an X-factor surfaced early the next morning. As I pulled into the gravel road, I noticed two trucks parked at the border of the public area. No matter, I thought. After all, it's public. But as I walked along the woods edge toward my listening spot, I saw a tent blind along a small finger of woods in the stubble field. That was a problem.

Scott had permission to hunt the property, and he said no one else should be there. However, I couldn't know whether the tent-blind hunters were trespassers or invited guests. And I sure wasn't going to knock on their tent in the dark and ask them.

Dejected, I hoofed across the field to the woods edge. I was nowhere near where I had planned to set up,

Lying on my belly in the wet grass, I could crawl to the lip of the field edge and send a hail of lead toward the gobbler. Yet I hesitate, considering the consequences. This is a new one. I have a turkey dead to rights, and I'm not shooting.

TES RANDLE JOLLY

Field Maneuvers, continued

but I figured I was far enough from the blind. Maybe I would hear another bird I could chase.

But true to my luck, the only turkey that gobbled that morning was the one we'd roosted. He started late but didn't stop for twenty minutes, until fly-down. Then, he flapped his wings, thundered off the ridge, and landed with a thud 80 yards away in the woods—right where I had planned to wait for him.

I dropped to my belly—there were no suitable trees around—in case the bird trotted down my gun barrel. Immediately, a box call sounded from the tent blind. The bird didn't respond, and I smiled silently. My smile widened when I heard several hens yelping and clucking where the gobbler had landed. The big boy was all henned-up. I probably wouldn't kill him, but I figured the tent-blinders wouldn't, either.

Across the Distance

Seconds later, a hen popped out of the woods 70-some steps away. Two more followed. The gobbler couldn't be far behind, and I wondered whether the tent-blind hunters could see him.

I figured the hens would feed toward the middle of the field and eventually drift into the woods. However, they swiftly made a large loop and ended up five steps away. One hen half-strutted and ran aggressively at the others, apparently trying to run them off. The other birds clucked and purred nervously as they evaded the aggressive hen.

Suddenly, the gobbler broke into view, strutting 65 steps away. His drumming filled the air, and his wings scraped loudly on the stubble as he pirouetted. Step by step, he drifted closer toward me and the hens.

This is a hunter-safety instructor's nightmare. Maybe my shot string wouldn't reach the blind, but I'm not taking that chance. At best, a ricochet or stray pellet would cause hard feelings. At worst . . . well, I have no choice. TES RANDLE JOLLY

"I don't believe this," I thought.

But as the box call sounded again, I realized my predicament. Barely visible in the early-morning light, the tent blind was about 125 steps across the field from me—and the gobbler was between us, in a direct line from my gun barrel to the other hunters. If the longbeard presented a shot, I'd be firing right at the guys in the blind.

Spur of the Moment

Minutes later, the situation hasn't changed. The turkey is somewhat closer, and I probably have to act now or forget about it. If I crawl slowly to the lip of the ridge, I can likely shoot the bird at 50 steps and deal with the consequences afterward.

But I have no idea who those guys in the blind are. Maybe it's the farmer and his grandson, or perhaps it's an out-of-town relative. Shooting this gobbler out from under them could jeopardize Scott's standing with the landowner.

And hell, that's not a consideration. Even if they're trespassers, this is a hunter-safety instructor's nightmare. Maybe my shot string wouldn't reach the blind, but I'm not taking that chance. At best, a ricochet or stray pellet would cause hard feelings. At worst . . . well, I have no choice.

The hens slowly drift away, and the gobbler follows, too far for me or the tent-blinders to shoot. I slip down the ridge and walk quickly through the woods edge, hoping to cut the birds off atop the hill. As I creep up the edge of public road, I see the hens pecking in a smaller stubble field—right by the parked trucks of the other hunters.

I crawl under the trucks and along a small tree line next to the field. The gobbler is about 70 steps away in the corner of the woods, strutting for a hen. I realize I'll never get closer than about 65 steps to him, so I roll over the road, slip into the woods, creep down the hill, and prepare to swing around from below. Just then, two deer jump from their beds and run at the turkeys. I set up and call, but it's finished. The gobbler and his harem are gone.

The Stomach Punch

I feel like I've been socked in the gut. I had that bird killed but couldn't shoot him. I think I did the right thing. After all, no turkey is worth any potentially unsafe action. Still, doubts linger. The gobbler is still out there, hopefully waiting for me next spring. I know I'll think of him often until then.

Notes from the Turkey Woods

The Decoy Deception

You never know where danger will arise in the turkey woods. Sometimes, it walks right to you in plain sight.

Years ago, a friend was turkey hunting at the farm of a mutual friend. He'd placed two or three decoys in the corner of a small stubble field, set up near a big double-trunked white oak and sat down to blind-call for a while.

After about an hour, he noticed a slight movement near the crest of the field about 80 steps away. He knew immediately that it wasn't a turkey, but that was about it. Soon, however, he realized two men were walking toward him. Thinking it might be the farmer and his farmhand, he stood and waved to them.

The men didn't see my friend, but they saw his decoys. One of them grabbed the other's arm and pointed. Then, he shouldered his shotgun and pointed it directly at my friend and his fake turkeys. Fearing a string of shot was on its way, my friend dove and rolled out of the way, yelling at the men so they wouldn't fire. Thankfully, they didn't.

Scared and steaming mad, my friend marched out to meet the intruders. He introduced himself, told them he had permission to hunt there, and asked them what the hell they were doing pointing a loaded shotgun at him from 70-some steps.

"Oh, I wasn't gonna shoot," one of the men said. "I was just looking at your decoys through my scope."

My friend told them that wasn't acceptable, either, and then asked if they had permission to be on the land.

"Well, we talked to one guy who said he thought the owner wouldn't mind," he said. "We're just gonna walk around for a while."

My friend's jaw dropped. Not only had the guys trespassed, ruined his hunt, and pointed a loaded gun at him, but they intended to stay!

He walked away without another word, grabbed his decoys, marched to the truck, and went home. As expected, the trespassers weren't there the next day, so he continued hunting the farm. But as he admitted later, he kept looking over his shoulder. !≮

"Oh, I wasn't gonna shoot," one of the men said. "I was just looking at your decoys through my scope."

CHAPTER 12

You must wear camo in the turkey woods, especially when chasing hard-hunted gobblers. Further, today's camo is the best concealment clothing ever produced.

Gotta Have It:
Turkey Gear

It was opening day in Alabama, one of the holiest days on a turkey hunter's calendar, and some fellow outdoor writers and I had joined two high-profile callers at a Black Belt lodge.

The first morning dawned cool, calm, and clear, and you simply knew a turkey would gobble when light started to streak the eastern sky. A lodge guide and I followed behind one of the callers and a writer as they slipped into a small clearing on a timbered island, and everyone had high hopes.

As cardinals began to sound off, the caller pulled an owl-hooter from his vest and blew an eight-note barred owl call. A gobbler blew up in response. But instead of tucking away his call and slipping toward the roosted bird, the caller stepped back toward the writer and held the hooter up in the moonlight.

"This is our latest model," he said. "It's new to the market this year, and it's going to be the hottest owl-hooter out there."

The writer nodded and then looked anxiously toward the turkey. In no hurry, the caller pocketed his hooter and slipped a diaphragm call into his cheek. He tree-yelped softly, and again, the bird jumped all over it.

"This is our new diaphragm call with a secret cutt," he whispered. "You can really hammer on it, but tone it down for soft clucks and purrs."

The writer stared blankly at the call. Seconds later, the caller pulled a friction call from his vest and popped a few soft clucks. The turkey went crazy, gobbling itself into a frenzy.

"This is our latest glass call," the caller said. "It has a special striker and can really reach out and touch birds."

The writer nodded again but said nothing. Eventually, the turkey flew down, the caller yelped it in, and the writer shot it at 20 steps. He and the caller were ecstatic because it had been a classic hunt.

After handshakes and back slaps, the writer suggested a photo session was in order. The caller, of course, agreed and began gathering all his gear for the picture.

"I didn't get a chance to use this," he said, holding up a box call. "This is our new . . . "

Sigh. Sometimes, turkey hunters take gear all too seriously. Of course, a big part of the caller's job was to promote the products his company made—especially when guiding a fellow who wrote turkey hunting stories for national magazines. But as any veteran hunter—including that gear-happy caller—will attest, you don't need to drag the kitchen sink into the woods to kill a turkey. The sport can be as gear-intensive as you want to make it.

I'm probably somewhere in the middle ground when it comes to turkey gear. I carry much more stuff than a minimalist, but I'm certainly no gadget guy, either. So here, in no particular order, are my suggestions and recommendations about must-have gear for turkey hunters. I'll also throw in information about some stuff you don't necessarily need but that might make your hunt a bit easier or more enjoyable.

Note: Because we've already covered calls and calling, I won't reiterate my thoughts on that. Suffice to say, you should carry several calls of various types because you never know which sound will fire turkeys up.

DUDED UP

For years, turkey hunters have debated the value of camouflage clothing. There's a great old story about a young turkey hunter talking with an old-timer. When the subject of camo arose, the old-timer scoffed.

"Shoot, sonny, we damn near wiped turkeys off the face of the earth while wearing bib overalls," he said.

True enough. It's also true that the best camouflage in the world won't do a thing if you move at an inopportune time. A gobbler will bust you double-quick.

But despite that, let's face it: you must wear camo in the turkey woods, especially when chasing hard-hunted gobblers. Further, today's camo is the best concealment clothing ever produced. The "Big Two" camouflage companies—Realtree and Mossy Oak—continue to push the limits on

What pattern should you wear? Honestly, they're all good and will hide you from a sharp-eyed longbeard (again, provided you don't move). Basically, try to match your camo pattern to the cover and terrain of your hunting area. If you hunt big woods, go with a timber pattern that has plenty of dark shadows. If you hunt the plains or open ag country, you'll want a lighter pattern that resembles grass or cattails.

Make sure you're camouflaged from head to toe, with a cap, facemask, gloves, shirt, and pants that hide your skin.

innovative patterns. And smaller yet reputable outfits such as Natgear and Skyline also produce great hunting wear.

What pattern should you wear? Honestly, they're all good and will hide you from a sharp-eyed longbeard (again, provided you don't move). Basically, try to match your camo pattern to the cover and terrain of your hunting area. If you hunt big woods, go with a timber pattern that has plenty of dark shadows. If you hunt the plains or open ag country, you'll want a lighter pattern that resembles grass or cattails. You get the idea.

In addition, make sure you're camouflaged from head to toe, with a cap, facemask, gloves, shirt, and pants that hide your skin.

Of course, your camo won't do much good if you can't get to your hunting area. And if you've ever spent a day traipsing up and down hardwood ridges, you know that good footwear is essential for turkey hunting. I won't get into individual brands of footwear. Basically, you want a boot that is light, durable, and comfortable, and you usually get what you pay for. Good ankle support is a must, especially if you're hunting hill country.

Also, tailor your boot selection to the climate. If you're hunting the last week of May in Kansas, you won't want a boot packed with Thinsulate. Conversely, that boot would serve you well if you're hunting Wisconsin's mid-April opener.

continued on page 181

BUT WHAT ABOUT DECOYS?

Depending on who you ask, turkey decoys are the greatest thing since the mouth call or the biggest scourge since blackhead disease.

They're probably somewhere between those extremes. But love them or hate them, no one can deny that decoys are integral turkey tools. And although I don't always use decoys, I always carry them—no exceptions.

The Number One problem with decoys is knowing when to use them and when to keep them in your vest. The answer lies in the nature of turkey decoys. They're not so much an attractant as they are a visual reassurance.

In spring hunting, you engage gobblers via sound by calling. Whether you answer a tom or get him to gobble, you're telling him there's a hen nearby that's ready to breed. If everything goes well, he'll come to check things out. Depending on the situation, decoys can reassure a gobbler that the hen is really there.

Sometimes, that reassurance is unnecessary. Remember that perfect setup we discussed earlier, where you won't see a gobbler—and vice versa—until he's in range. Ideally, there will be a small terrain rise, brushy obstruction, a bend in a logging road, or something similar that prevents the gobbler from seeing the source of the calling until he pops his head up at 30 steps.

In such situations, you don't need a decoy. The bird cannot see the hen, but because of the terrain or other factors, he knows that's not unnatural. When he pops over a rise or around a bend in the logging road, he'll almost always stop and crane his neck to look for the source of the calling, which should then be visible. If he doesn't see it, he'll usually leave fairly quickly. However, you'll no doubt have sent a swarm of shot his way by then.

Of course, as we also mentioned, you can't always find those perfect setups. Turkeys often use open areas—meadows, open bottoms, pastured woods, agricultural fields, and open benches of mature timber—where they can see long distances. If a longbeard comes to your calling at these spots, he might approach to within 80 yards, look for the source of the calling—he'll know exactly where it came from—note the absence of a hen and high-tail it elsewhere.

So in open spots where you—and turkeys—can see long distances, it's wise to use decoys. If a gobbler approaches and sees a hen or breeding flock near the source of the calling, it tells him everything is natural, and that the hot little hen is right where she should be. That doesn't ensure he'll come in, but it helps.

You probably know the basic decoy drill: set up one to three decoys 20 or so steps from your setup. For safety reasons, make sure they're at somewhat of an angle from you. And if you use a jake decoy, make sure it's facing you so an aggressive gobbler will go beak to beak with it.

But What About Decoys? continued

That's good advice, but decoy placement is a bit more involved. Many hunters place their hen decoys low to the ground, like a hen in breeding position. If you add a jake decoy to the mix, approaching gobblers sometimes go crazy. Later in the season, try placing your hen decoy so it's somewhat obscured, whether partially behind brush or just over a small terrain rise. That often plays on a gobbler's curiosity.

Of course, motion is a great attractant. Whether the wind moves your decoys back and forth, or you use motion decoys, movement adds an element of realism. Gobblers that see a hen decoy shift slightly in the breeze often break and come right in, convinced the plastic hen is the real thing. During windy days, decoys might move too much. Place another stake or small twig next to the decoy so it doesn't blow over and its range of motion is limited.

Many hunters use the standard two- or three-decoy setup early in the season but abandon decoys later, believing gobblers become "decoy shy." True, longbeards sometimes shy away from decoys. However, that's often a function of turkey nature vs. learned behavior.

Often, two-year-olds or other subdominant turkeys avoid jake decoys. They might see the white head and red neck of the jake decoy and assume it's another gobbler. Not wanting to get their butt kicked again, the birds stay at a respectful distance. Also, groups of jakes often gang up on longbeards, so a gobbler that's been whipped by a band of thugs might avoid a jake decoy.

Nonetheless, anyone who has experienced a successful hunt with a jake decoy won't forget it. Gobblers often react aggressively to jake fakes, posturing and strutting in the face of the decoys, and sometimes attacking and flogging them. Even folks who have seen birds spook from jake decoys agree that they work more often than not.

There's another reason gobblers might avoid decoys: some are just obstinate. They might see a decoy and hear the calling, but won't approach within range. Why? They simply expect the hen to come to them, which is what usually happens.

Of course, it's reasonable to assume a gobbler that has been spooked or shot at when coming to decoys might not rush to them again. However, in most cases, a turkey that avoids fakes is likely just being a fickle turkey.

Veteran hunters usually don't abandon decoys late in the season, but as mentioned, they might pare down their spread, using just one hen instead of two hens and a jake. But often, the traditional spreads work until the season's final day.

You don't have to stake out your decoys every time you set up on a gobbler this spring. But when you do, be confident they're helping your cause. And when you stare down your shotgun barrel at a strutting gobbler, smile and know you've played the decoy game right.

Upland-style walking boots are my choice for most situations, but I always make sure to have a good pair of knee-high rubber boots along if I'm hunting swampy country or must walk through an ankle-high alfalfa field in the morning. Swampers aren't as comfortable as walking boots, but believe me, walking boots aren't that comfortable when your feet are soaked.

If we're toting loads of gear into the field, we'll need something in which to carry it. Turkey vests fit the bill perfectly. They come in numerous configurations, but the concept remains the same: they provide several pockets and compartments for calls and other goodies, and usually feature a flip-down cushion to save your fanny on long setups.

Vests can be as spartan or minimal as you like. Usually, I opt for the king-sized models with umpteen pockets. That way, I can carry every call I think I'll need, plus food, water, decoys, and other tools. Just make sure a vest fits your needs.

You want a boot that is light, durable, and comfortable, and you usually get what you pay for. Good ankle support is a must, especially if you're hunting hill country.

I like vests with adjustable buckles in front, which makes them much more comfortable when you're walking. Also, though most vests have cushions for your tush, some don't provide much padding. If you plan to sit for a while, consider bringing an air cushion or a tire inner tube, or sew extra padding into your cushion.

Some vests feature support systems that let you sit comfortably without back support. These are very handy when you're hunting open or sparsely timbered areas and must set up without an ideal tree. The support systems add some weight and bulk, but it's well worth it, especially if you've ever had to sit Indian-style while waiting on a gobbler.

You can fill your turkey vest with all sorts of fun stuff if you want. Calls, shells, gloves, a facemask, and water are absolutes. You'll also want to carry a good pair of binoculars. These add weight and might seem like a pain, but they pay off big-time, even if you hunt large timbered areas. Also, you'll want to carry a small ratchet-style clippers to quickly prune brush and small limbs at your setups. In addition, I like to bring a turkey tote, which is nothing more than a small strap that helps you carry a gobbler out of the woods. You don't need this, of course, but it sure beats wrapping your hands around a bird's legs until the tendons in your forearm bulge out.

No matter where you hunt, you'll want to carry a compass. If you're on large or unfamiliar tracts, you might want a global positioning system (GPS) unit. Spending some money and carrying that extra piece of equipment just might prevent you from getting lost.

Of course, if you plan to be out all day, you'll want some food, too. Jerky or snack-sized candy bars provide quick pick-me-ups and don't take up too much space.

GUNS AND AMMO

Hunters often ask what constitutes the "ultimate" turkey gun. Really, the answer is simple: one that functions flawlessly and consistently kills turkeys.

Okay, it's more involved than that. Myriad considerations are involved in choosing the ideal turkey gun. Many are personal preferences, but others are based on common sense and in-the-field experience.

There's nothing wrong with a good-patterning 20- or 16-gauge shotgun for turkey hunting. However, if you're seeking optimum performance, your weapon should be a 12- or 10-gauge. And because the big 10s can be heavy and awkward afield, you can probably eliminate them from the equation, too.

Hunters often ask what constitutes the "ultimate" turkey gun. The answer is simple: one that functions flawlessly and consistently kills turkeys.

Your 12-gauge should be chambered for 3- or even $3^1/2$-inch shells. Do you need $3^1/2$-inch magnums to kill a turkey? No. However, some guns pattern better with $3^1/2$-inch shells, so it never hurts to have that option.

Short barrels are a big advantage in the turkey woods. They make your gun somewhat lighter and much more maneuverable. Most specialized turkey guns feature 22- to 24-inch barrels.

Also, your gun must be camouflaged to some extent. It doesn't have to sport the latest pattern from major manufacturers, but it should at least have a matte finish or be fitted with camo tape to eliminate glare and reflection.

You'll probably want a recoil pad, too—not so much for the woods, but for the patterning range. It's amazing how firing a few 3-inch rounds can pound your shoulder and cause flinching.

Should you go with a pump, autoloader, or double-barreled gun? You can make cases for each. Autoloaders reduce recoil somewhat and eliminate the need to shuck out a spent hull. However, even the best might jam at some point. Pumps are ultra-reliable and light to carry. That lightness, however, translates to a slight increase in recoil.

Few folks carry side-by-sides or over-and-unders in the woods, but double-guns have one huge advantage: two barrels, each of which can be

Short barrels are a big advantage in the turkey woods. They make your gun somewhat lighter and much more maneuverable. Most specialized turkey guns feature 22- to 24-inch barrels.

fitted with a different choke. Double-barrel fans often use a super-full turkey choke in one barrel for shots 30 yards and farther and a modified choke for close shots. If you've ever missed a turkey at 15 steps or blown a baseball-size hole in his neck, you realize the advantage of having a second barrel with an open choke.

Your choke-and-load combination might be the most important element of the turkey-gun equation. With the right mix, you can throw beautiful patterns out to 50 steps. Without a good combo, you might miss or cripple turkeys.

The best turkey shotshells are 3-inch loads of $1^3/_4$ to $2^1/_2$ ounces of No. 4, 5, or 6 lead or No. 4, 5, 6, or $7^1/_2$ Hevi-shot. Fired through the correct choke, any of these loads will smoke a gobbler.

Some folks like No. 6 shot because it provides greater pellet count and better pattern density. Others prefer the increased downrange energy of No. 4 shot, and some go with No. 5s, because they split the difference.

However, many folks don't take time to determine the best choke for their chosen load. They might decide on No. 5 shot and then screw in a factory or aftermarket choke, throw a couple of patterns at the range and go hunting. Big mistake. Determine a shot size based on their relative merits. But then, custom-fit your choke so the shotshell performs well.

Match the constriction of your choke with the size of shot you intend to shoot. Smaller shot works best out of tighter chokes. Larger shot performs well out of slightly looser chokes. If you're using No. 6 shot, for example, you'll likely get great patterns with an ultra-tight .660-constriction choke. If you're using No. 4 shot, you'll want to use a less-constrictive model, such as a .680. For No. 5 shot, split the difference.

Also, consider an after-market choke. Many factory chokes perform well, but your gun will usually shoot better with a precision-machined after-market model. When you think you have the ideal shot-and-choke marriage, hit the range.

Shooting a gobbler might be the least difficult part of turkey hunting. Still, it's easy to miss a bird. Any turkey hunter who says he's never missed a longbeard is a liar or hasn't hunted much.

How can you miss a twenty-pound bird that's usually standing still? Because shooting a turkey gun is more like shooting a rifle than a scatter-gun. You're firing a shot pattern a little larger than a softball at about 20 steps. If you're off by a couple of inches, or a gobbler ducks his head a split-second before you shoot, you'll miss him.

Further, a standard shotgun bead—or even a front and rear bead—pretty much obscures a gobbler farther than 40 steps. When you put the bead on the head or neck of a bird at 40-plus steps, you're basically guessing. You wouldn't fire a big-game rifle without a sight, so your turkey gun should be similarly equipped with a sight or scope.

Iron or fiber-optic sights work well. They're easy to sight in, provide pinpoint accuracy, and don't add bulk like a scope. Light-gathering fiber-optic models are especially nice in the haze of early morning. If there's one knock against such sights it's that they can snag or break on brush or limbs.

Scopes are becoming more common on turkey guns. Most hunters prefer red-dot models, but some still like cross-hairs. Almost all scope fans use models with little or no magnification. The down side of scopes is that they can be knocked out of alignment. Check your scope often to make sure it's dead on.

It takes time and work to fine-tune your ultimate turkey hunting shotgun, but the results are worthwhile. Confident in your equipment, you can stare down your barrel at a gobbler without worrying about anything except your pounding heart.

Notes from the Turkey Woods

A Lot or A Little? Two Views

Years ago, during several trips to Missouri, I witnessed a study in the minimalist and gear-nut approaches to turkey hunting.

The minimalist was Don Shipp, three-time world-champion caller and perhaps the all-time great turkey killer. Every morning, Shipp threw on his camo, laced up his boots, donned a ball cap, grabbed a couple of diaphragm calls, slung his shotgun over his back, and hit the woods. That was the extent of his equipment.

"I've never worn a turkey vest," he said one day. "Never needed one. Every now and then, I'll throw a slate or a glass call in one of my pockets, but I really don't use it much, either."

Of course, there aren't many wild turkeys that can make hen calls as pretty as those Shipp produces. Further, you'll hunt many years and cover a lot of ground before you find anyone who matches Shipp in woodsmanship and turkey hunting knowledge, so his spartan approach might be extreme.

Conversely, Shipp and I often shared a camp with an outdoors writer who usually carried the turkey vest of all turkey vests. I'm not sure what he carried in that thing. Oh, he had loads of calls, to be sure. And water. And food. And extra cushions. And perhaps some gold coins or something. One day, I returned from a hunt, threw my vest on the porch and complained about how heavy it was. He chuckled, picked up his vest and said in his best Southern drawl, "Now, this is a turkey vest." My arm lurched downward with the weight. Good grief! He must have had thirty-some pounds of gear in that tattered old vest.

"What all do you have in there?" I asked.

"Well, just everything I need," he replied.

I couldn't argue.

But I guessed then that "need" varied greatly with personal preference.

The amount of gear you tote into the woods is based on personal preference. Some folks do well with little gear, but others like to tote everything they might need.

EPILOGUE

It's been said many times, but it's true: No other activity comes close to the up-and-down, boom-or-bust roller coaster of events and emotions of turkey hunting. Mark and Terry Drury sum this up with words of advice their uncle Marvin gave them long ago: "Some days, you can't do nothin' wrong, and some days, you can't do nothin' right."

It has always been that way, and it will always be so. That's a big reason why turkey hunting is so enthralling yet frustrating. However, I suspect that as the amount of generally accessible hunting land shrinks and interest in turkey hunting increases, folks will find themselves dealing more often with pressured turkeys. As such, I'm guessing the spring roller coaster might be a bit more exciting in years to come.

In a way, I think this isn't all bad. If interest in turkey hunting were waning, I'd be worried. But it's certainly not. The gobbler bug has infected many heretofore disinterested nonhunters. Those folks are now part of a devoted cadre of spring zealots, and such numbers and passion represents a powerful lobby. That is, the more folks who care about turkeys and their habitat, the better for the bird.

Of course, increased—or, more accurately, increasingly focused—pressure probably isn't what you want to see when you park your truck some beautiful moonlit April morning. Still, I suspect we'll all have to face such scenarios.

I hope this book will help you deal with the social and practical aspects of hunting pressured turkeys. If I were to "bottom-line" it, I'd tell you to be patient, use your head, remember that pressured turkeys are still just turkeys, and to be safe, courteous, and respectful toward your fellow hunters. You'll find that hunting pressured turkeys isn't terribly different than hunting their uninitiated brethren.

Of course, if you can find and access unpressured birds, do it! But don't get upset if you find you're not alone in the woods. After all, I'd rather hunt pressured birds than not hunt at all.

Years ago, a fellow told me he didn't care if he ever killed another spring gobbler, but he had to hunt them. I'm not quite to that stage, but I'm getting there. It's not so much that I need to sling gobblers over my shoulder several times each spring. I just need to hear them gobble, play cat-and-mouse with them, and experience the joyous insanity that is turkey hunting.

If I need to share the woods with fellow hunters to do that—and chase pressured turkeys in the process—so be it. It's still one of the most rewarding pursuits I can imagine.

Hunting pressured turkeys might be tougher than chasing their unpressured brethren, but it's still one of the most rewarding pursuits the author can imagine.
TES RANDLE JOLLY

INDEX